DESIGN
SENSITIVITY

To C. Michael York,
who won't recognize his hand in it
but provided the initial spark nonetheless.

DESIGN SENSITIVITY
Statistical Power for Experimental Research

Mark W. Lipsey

SAGE Publications
International Educational and Professional Publisher
Newbury Park   London   New Delhi

For information address:

SAGE Publications, Inc.
2455 Teller Road
Newbury Park, California 91320
E-mail: order@sagepub.com

SAGE Publications Ltd.
6 Bonhill Street
London EC2A 4PU
United Kingdom

SAGE Publications India Pvt. Ltd.
M-32 Market
Greater Kailash I
New Delhi 110 048 India

Printed in the United States of America

Library of Congress Cataloging-in-Publication Data

Lipsey, Mark W.
  Design sensitivity: statistical power for experimental research /
  Mark W. Lipsey.
    p.   cm.—
  Includes bibliographical references.
  ISBN 0-8039-3062-3—ISBN 0-8039-3063-1 (pbk.)
    1. Social service—Statistical methods I. Title. II. Series:
HV29.L57   1990
362.3'072—dc20   89-37647
                                                             CIP

00   01   13   12   11   10

Contents

Acknowledgments

This book began with a riddle. After evaluation of a number of delinquency prevention programs, I concluded, despite initial skepticism, that they did indeed have some positive benefit. The research literature on delinquency treatment, however, reported such a preponderance of null results that virtually all reviewers reached much less favorable conclusions. Attempting to account for this discrepancy led me to closer examination of the methods and practices characteristic of treatment effectiveness research in juvenile justice and other practical domains. I have learned much from that endeavor, and this book is an attempt to share with a wider audience some of what I have learned.

Much of my riddling has been conducted at taxpayers' expense, and credit for any good that has come of it should go first to those stalwart public servants at the Los Angeles County Regional Criminal Justice Planning Board, the Los Angeles County Youth Services Network, the National Institute of Justice, and the National Institute of Mental Health, as well as to the Russell Sage Foundation, all of whom have supported my research on juvenile delinquency treatment over the years.

This book might never have developed beyond the outline stage without the steady encouragement and counsel of Leonard Bickman and Debra Rog, editors of the Sage Applied Social Research Methods Series. I am immensely grateful for their valuable suggestions, patient pacing of my efforts, and exceptional good grace (when it became apparent that the manuscript had grown too long to be published as part of their series). Preparation of this manuscript was also aided by the comments of Zoe Barley, Robert Boruch, David Cordray, Amiram Vinokur, Susan Winter, and William Yeaton. I owe special thanks to David Cordray and Robert Boruch, who generally had better ideas about what I should say than I did (and didn't mind telling me so!). Jane Gray, whose administrative and secretarial talents have sustained the Claremont Graduate School Psychology Department for many years, assisted with her usual, but no less remarkable,

7

mastery of both balky word processing equipment and testy authors. Finally, my thanks go to the graduate students in my research methods classes who, knowing this book was written for them, kept prodding me to do a better job of it.

Part I

Statistical Power in Treatment Effectiveness Research

Of the many different types of research situations in the behavioral sciences, this book is concerned with those that study the effects of deliberate intervention. We do something and we want to know if it makes a difference. A researcher, for instance, might expose subjects to stressful noise to investigate the effects on their ability to solve anagrams. A psychotherapist might study the efficacy of systematic desensitization for reducing the symptoms of triskaidekaphobia (fear of the number 13). A school might evaluate the success of a drug education program in preventing substance abuse among students. A policymaker might ask for evidence that altering the tax rate on gasoline will discourage consumption. The research domain encompassing such inquiries will be referred to in this volume as "treatment effectiveness research."

A particular focus of this volume is *applied* treatment effectiveness research, that which investigates intervention of practical rather than primarily theoretical interest. Such research often involves ill-defined and complex treatments whose effects must, of necessity, be studied under field conditions rather than in the controlled environment of the laboratory. Under such circumstances it may be a considerable challenge to achieve the basic elements of experimental design. Because of the practical importance of investigating promising interventions for real problems, however, finding ways to meet such challenges deserves the best efforts of researchers.

Whether in the laboratory or the field, one of the more important challenges for the treatment effectiveness researcher is designing research that will have sufficient sensitivity to detect those effects it purports to investigate. The sensitivity of a research design is determined by many factors—sample size, reliability and validity of measures, experimental error, subject variability, strength and integrity of treatment, type of statistical analysis, and so forth. The end result, however, is a data set upon which the statistical significance of treatment effects can be tested using procedures that have a high level of statistical power. Design sensitivity, in other words, results in data that are likely to yield statistical significance if, in fact, the treatment under investigation is effective.

Part I of this volume introduces the concept of design sensitivity and explains statistical power and the elements that determine it. Chapter 1 reviews the issues of validity and sensitivity in experimental research and illustrates the many factors that degrade sensitivity. In Chapter 2, statistical power is defined and the special problems it poses for treatment effectiveness research are examined. The most problematic aspect of statistical power is the effect size, a statistical index of the magnitude of effect an experiment is designed to detect. Chapter 3 is devoted to discussion of the effect-size parameter and various approaches to assessing it. Chapter 4, the last in Part I, describes how statistical power can be estimated for various statistical tests of the mean difference between a treatment group and a control group on an outcome measure of interest.

1. Treatment Effectiveness Research and Design Sensitivity

The conventional research paradigm for treatment effectiveness research is experimental design, and its basic elements are well-known: selection of subjects and assignment of them to treatment and control conditions, preferably using a random procedure; application of the intervention of interest to the treatment group but not to the control group (independent variable); experimental control of the research situation to ensure that there are no differences between the treatment and control conditions other than the intervention; measurement of selected outcomes for both groups (dependent variables); and statistical analysis to determine if the groups differ on those dependent variable measures. This volume assumes that the reader is familiar with the elements of experimental design and the logic which leads from that design to conclusions about the effectiveness of treatment.

The object of experimental design is to come as close as possible to creating a situation in which the *only* difference between the treatment and control conditions is the intervention of interest. When this is accomplished we can interpret the differences between those conditions on measured dependent variables as effects of the intervention. Ensuring that the researcher is able to detect any real difference between treatment and control, that is, the treatment *effect,* is the concern of the remainder of this volume. To simplify the discussion and better expose the underlying concepts, we will, in most instances, assume a prototypical experimental design consisting of a single treatment group (subjects in the intervention condition) compared with a single control group (subjects in the nonintervention condition) on one or more measured dependent variables. This prototypical design is simpler than might actually be used in many instances of practical treatment effectiveness research. The principles that apply to it, however, are general and, for the most part, easily extend to more complex designs.

Using experimental design to investigate treatment effects is much like using radar to detect incoming aircraft. There are many ways to miss what is really there and "find" what is not there. With radar, for example, the equipment may not be pointed in the right direction or switched on at the right time. It may not be sensitive enough to detect craft below a certain threshold size or it may be so sensitive to background noise that real signals are difficult to pick out. Additionally, it may respond to extraneous objects (e.g., clouds, weather balloons) as if they were the craft of interest or fail to respond to some craft that are of interest (e.g., those in the wrong orientation or constructed of nonmetallic materials).

With experimental design and treatment effects, we can classify broadly the many ways to go wrong under the labels of *sensitivity* and *validity*. Sensitivity refers to the likelihood that an effect, if present, will be detected. Validity refers to the likelihood that what is detected is, in fact, the effect of interest. This volume is about the problem of sensitivity but, before plunging into that topic, a few words about validity are in order.

The Problem of Validity

What we mean by validity in experimental design is that the picture we get of the effects of treatment from comparing experimental conditions on selected dependent measures corresponds to the "real" effects in the circumstances investigated. The concept of validity has been usefully and influentially elaborated in the writings of Campbell and Stanley (1966) and Cook and Campbell (1979). They differentiated four types of validity, one of which—statistical conclusion validity—will be discussed later since it is an aspect of what we are calling "sensitivity" in this context.

The other types of validity—internal validity, construct validity, and external validity—apply to the interpretation of an experimental effect, that is, a difference between a treatment and a control condition on a dependent measure. Internal validity refers to the question of whether the treatment, taken as a global manipulation or operationalization, was the source of a given effect in contrast to some other factor in the situation that might have caused it. Construct validity refers to the correspondence between the treatment and outcome concepts that motivate the research and the particular manipulations or operationalizations used to represent them in an experiment. External validity refers to the correspondence between the results of a given experiment and what would occur in other situations more or less similar to those studied but not actually included in the experiment.

These concepts of validity are discussed much more thoroughly elsewhere (see Cook & Campbell, 1979). For present purposes, we want only to emphasize that the validity of an experimental design for assessing treatment effectiveness depends very much upon how that design is constructed. Internal validity, for instance, depends principally upon random assignment of subjects to treatment versus control groups and the maintenance of uniform experimental conditions that differ only on the treatment variable. Construct validity requires thoughtful operationalization of experimental conditions and dependent variables to represent adequately the question at issue. External validity relies on a clear definition of the circumstances to which the experimental results are to generalize and appropriate sampling of subjects, settings, times, and the like. Failure to take proper care in these matters can produce experimental results that are biased, misleading, misrepresentative, irrelevant, and, in short, just plain wrong.

Let us suppose, however, (as we will throughout this volume) that an experiment has been designed carefully to maintain, as well as possible under the research circumstances, appropriate internal validity, construct validity, and external validity. Does it then follow that it will find whatever treatment effects are really there? The answer, unfortunately, is an emphatic "No!" An experimental design must be sensitive as well as valid. If treatment effects of meaningful magnitude are below the threshold of what a particular experimental design can reliably detect, no amount of improvement in its internal, construct, and external validity will rescue it from error.

Issues of validity, especially internal validity, are generally given a great deal of attention in the design of treatment effectiveness research. Issues of sensitivity are given comparatively little attention—indeed, they are widely neglected. If this were because sensitivity was relatively unimportant or because adequate sensitivity was routinely attained, that neglect might be understandable. Such is not the case, however. It is easy to show (and will be shown later) that most treatment effectiveness research is designed at such a low level of sensitivity that it has little likelihood of detecting the effects it purports to investigate. This volume, therefore, will deal with design sensitivity—what it is and how to ensure that it is adequate in treatment effectiveness research. It will assume that a study is otherwise designed to be valid. After all, it makes little sense to design a sensitive experiment that lacks validity, just as it makes little sense to construct a valid experiment that is insensitive.

The Problem of Sensitivity

We can think of sensitivity in treatment effectiveness research as the ability to detect a real contrast or difference between experimental conditions on some characteristic of interest. If the research has been designed to be valid, that contrast or difference will represent the effect of the treatment under investigation. What, then, determines our ability to detect it? The answer, in brief, is *relative variability*—how much "noise" or "scatter" or, more precisely, "error" there is in the dependent variable scores within experimental conditions in relationship to the difference between the conditions.

The role of relative variability in detecting contrast can be illustrated as follows. Suppose we are standing on a hill overlooking a road, trying to judge which of two groups of travelers, the X's or the O's, is farther along. If there is no variability within each group in progress down the road, as when they are walking abreast, we see something like panel A in Figure 1.1. In this case, the contrast between the groups is easy to detect (our eye is the instrument) and we see that the O's are in the lead.

If, however, the members of each group are scattered about, we may see something like panel B in Figure 1.1. In this case it is much more difficult to judge the difference in progress between the two groups despite the fact that the *average* location of each group is exactly the same as in the previous case.

As noted, however, the role of variability is a relative one. What is too much depends upon the size of the contrast we are trying to detect. In the example above, for instance, if our traveling groups have the same scatter as in panel B but are farther apart (as in panel C), the difference once again becomes easy to observe.

In treatment effectiveness research, the problem is complicated by variability introduced through sampling, experimental procedure, measurement, and a variety of other such factors. For example, to the extent that different samples from the population of interest will vary even in the absence of treatment effects, sampling error blurs any distinction between groups. To the extent that each member of each group is not treated the same during the experimental procedures and thus may respond differently, experimental error further obscures any contrast. To the extent that the measurement of the outcomes of interest does not produce consistent results for each individual, measurement error contributes additional fuzziness. And so on.

More generally, the sensitivity of an experimental design to a treatment effect depends upon the following six factors:

a) Effect size: The magnitude of the "real" effect to be detected.
b) Subject heterogeneity: Individual differences among members of the relevant population on the dependent variable of interest.

A. Two groups of travelers walking abreast:

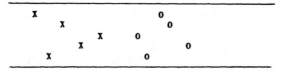

B. Same average difference between groups as above but travelers scattered:

C. Same scatter within groups as above but greater average distance between groups:

Figure 1.1: Illustration of the Role of Relative Variability in Detecting Contrast

    c) Sample size: The size of the sample taken from the population to constitute the experimental groups.

    d) Experimental error: Procedural variation in the way members of the experimental groups are treated during the research.

    e) Measurement: Muted or inconsistent response of the measurement instrument to the outcome of interest.

    f) Data analysis: The inherent power of the statistical data analysis technique employed to test the difference between experimental groups.

For those who are not thoroughly familiar with these concepts, a somewhat more realistic illustration may be helpful.

Pizza and soda. Suppose that we are interested in whether a diet of pizza and soda will produce more weight gain among college sophomores than will a normal diet. Following conventional experimental design, we plan to give one group of sophomores only pizza and soda for a month and another, equivalent group only a "normal" diet of college cafeteria food for that same period, then compare the mean bodyweight of the two groups.

We recognize that there are too many college sophomores in the country to use all of them in the experiment, so we draw a sample. At this point, we encounter the role of sample size in our ability to detect any differences in weight gain. At the extreme, if we were to select randomly only one sophomore for the normal diet and one for pizza and soda, we might (by chance) get, say, an active athletic female in one condition and a sedentary, lethargic male in the other. These differences in metabolism and activity level might so overshadow even a large effect of pizza and soda that we would be unable to detect it.

As we draw larger random samples, each group is more likely to be representative of the population and less likely to be atypical, and therefore the two groups are more likely to be similar on all relevant characteristics at the beginning of the experiment. Correspondingly, the less likelihood there is of any initial chance differences between our experimental groups to mask or spuriously enhance differences produced by treatment and the better able we are to detect the effects of treatment. This circumstance reflects the role of sample size in reducing sampling error and increasing the sensitivity of the design to treatment effects.

Consider now the closely related matter of the natural variability on the characteristic of interest (bodyweight) in the population. If all college sophomores weighed exactly the same, to the ounce, there would be correspondingly little variation in weight within our research samples. With so little variation, any difference in weight resulting from the different diets would be easy to observe, rather like the groups of travelers walking abreast in the earlier example. College sophomores do not all weigh the same, however. In fact, there is a fair amount of natural heterogeneity on this variable. The greater the heterogeneity, the more difficult it will be to detect a given difference between the groups resulting from difference in diet, and the less sensitive the experiment will be.

One way to improve the sensitivity of the design in response to subject heterogeneity is to cluster ("stratify" or "block") all sophomores of similar weight into subgroups within each experimental condition before comparing them. For example, we could take those subjects in the 95 to 100-pound range before treatment and compare the subsequent weights of those who received normal diets with those who ate the pizza and soda. We could make a similar comparison for those initially in the 100- to 105-pound bracket, 105-110, and so forth. Within each bracket, differences due to diet will be easier to detect because of the reduced variability in initial weight. Pooling the results from the many brackets causes little effective reduction in total sample size, and the overall experiment gains sensitivity. Variations on this approach to the control of subject heterogeneity include such adjustments to design format and statistical analysis as blocking, repeated measures designs, and analysis of covariance.

Having considered the nature of the research samples and the parent population from which they are drawn, let us move on to examine the experimental intervention itself. One obvious factor in our ability to detect bodyweight differences resulting from a pizza and soda diet is how big those differences really are. If a month of pizza and soda results in, say, a 50-pound weight gain relative to a normal diet, the difference will be readily apparent even in a fairly crude experimental design. If, on the other hand, the actual effect is only one pound, it may be difficult to detect under any practical research circumstances.

On the surface it may appear that there is little the researcher can do about the actual size of the effect under investigation. More reflection, however, reveals that the treatment effect will be at least partly a function of how the researcher implements it and, for that matter, how the contrasting control condition is implemented. The effect of the pizza and soda diet, for instance, will depend on the quantity of these delicacies that are ingested. If the treatment condition is limited to modest quantities, little weight gain may result even though larger quantities might, in fact, yield such gain. Moreover, even if unlimited quantities were provided, if the quality were so low as to be unattractive, atypically small amounts might be eaten (who wants cold pizza and flat soda?). Correspondingly, if the conditions arranged by the researcher somehow encouraged the control subjects to eat more or less of the normal diet than they might otherwise, the contrast between treatment and control is altered.

At issue here is the strength of the treatment or the size of the "dose" implemented in the experiment. Given the potential for an effect, stronger treatments should produce larger effects that can be more easily detected in experimental research. A researcher must give careful consideration to what treatment dose might reasonably be expected to produce detectable effects as well as to what dose is of practical or theoretical interest in the study context. Furthermore, once the appropriate treatment and control doses are defined, the researcher must ensure that they are actually delivered at the prescribed level.

A closely related consideration is the variability in the treatment and control conditions implemented and variability in other research procedures that may affect the outcome. Variable conditions are likely to produce variable results and, as noted earlier, greater variability within groups makes differences between groups harder to detect. If, for instance, the quantity or quality of food available varied considerably for different individuals within the experimental groups, any resulting variability in their bodyweights would contribute to the dispersion that could mask overall differences between the groups. Other procedural variation such as differences in the instructions given to subjects, the timing of meals, the circumstances of measurement, and so forth could have similar effects.

Procedural consistency in such research circumstances is usually referred to as experimental control. In the ideal experiment, each subject within a given experimental condition is treated exactly the same on all matters that may affect the study results so that the procedures themselves do not introduce unwanted variability into those results. An additional element of experimental control is to treat the subjects in different experimental conditions exactly the same except for the treatment itself. This enhances the validity of the experiment while also reducing the role of extraneous factors that might make treatment effects more difficult to detect.

Once the treatment and control regimens have run their course, the relevant dependent variable (bodyweight in this case) must be measured. Not surprisingly, the nature and circumstances of that measurement have a great deal to do with the sensitivity of the experiment to treatment effects. Consider first the matter of the responsiveness of the measurement instrument to the characteristic of interest. To be slightly absurd, if bodyweight were measured with a yardstick, any difference between the experimental groups would certainly not be detected. The measuring instrument must have validity—it must measure the characteristic of interest and not something else altogether. Even a valid instrument, however, may not be sufficiently responsive to the quantities at issue. If, for example, we attempted to weigh the college sophomores using the truck scales found on interstate highways, we would not likely find any effects. Truck scales are indeed valid instruments for measuring weight, but they are not sensitive to differences in the weight range that is relevant to our diet experiment. A related concern is whether the instrument is equally sensitive over the entire range of subject bodyweights. A scale that did not read weights over 100 pounds (or under 100 pounds), for instance, would be incapable of responding to bodyweight changes for some subjects (known generally as "ceiling" and "floor" effects in measurement).

Another way in which dependent measures can be insensitive to treatment effects is through unreliability—random error in the measured values such as is revealed when repeated measurement of the same quantity gives inconsistent results. Suppose, for instance, that the college sophomores in our experiment were weighed with an electronic scale which had a faulty transistor that caused the readings to fluctuate widely. Or perhaps it might be unduly sensitive to irrelevant factors such as humidity or temperature. The result is that the unreliability of the measurement instrument itself adds variability to the scores that are being compared for treatment and control groups. As seen previously, such variability reduces the ability of the experiment to detect differences.

Note that while some measurement unreliability may be inherent in the instrument itself, some may also be closely connected with procedural variability in the application of the instrument, an aspect of general experimental control. If the measurement procedure is not uniform—for example, sometimes weighing the sophomores with their shoes on and sometimes off—variability is introduced into the scores in ways virtually indistinguishable from whatever unreliability is inherent in the instrument.

Finally, the experiment comes down to a statistical analysis of the scores for the treatment group and the control group to determine if there is a statistically significant difference (greater than expected from sampling error) between them. Any such analysis involves the adoption of certain assumptions about the properties of the variables, groups, and so forth and a corresponding statistical "test" appropriate to those assumptions. There is often more than one defensible statistical test for experimental data, and each may vary in its conclusions with regard to whether the difference between two sets of dependent variable scores is statistically significant.

We might compare the posttreatment bodyweights of the pizza-eating versus normal sophomores, for example, using a Chi-square test (dichotomizing weight, say, at the grand median), a Mann-Whitney U test, a t-test, or an analysis of variance (not to mention a host of other obscure possibilities). While some of these are virtually interchangeable, others are not. Moreover, for each procedure we might choose either a "one-tailed" or a "two-tailed" test depending upon what statistical hypothesis we judged most relevant to our interest. The different choices that might be made on these matters can yield different statistical conclusions about treatment effects. Design sensitivity is enhanced when the researcher selects the most sensitive test for which the necessary assumptions can be met.

We see from this example that at every step in the process of conducting treatment effectiveness research, the researcher makes choices that affect the ability of the study to detect treatment effects. The sensitivity of a research design to such effects, therefore, is not a function of a single element of the design (such as sample size) but rather a characteristic of the entire research package. The net result is what is called *design sensitivity* in this volume—the ability of a treatment effectiveness study, including its plan, implementation, and statistical analysis, to detect treatment effects.

The goal of this volume is to help a researcher "tune" experimental design to maximize sensitivity or, at the very least, to ensure that the research meets some minimal standard of sensitivity appropriate to its purpose. Before close examination of the practical issues related to design sensitivity can be made, however, it is necessary to have a more refined framework for describing and assessing the end result—a high probability of detecting a given magnitude of effect if it exists. This brings us to the topic of *statistical power*, the concept that will provide the idiom for the more detailed discussion of design sensitivity that follows in the subsequent chapters of this volume.

Statistical Power

In the final analysis treatment effectiveness research comes down to just that: analysis (data analysis, that is). After all the planning, implementation, and paperwork, the researcher is left with a set of data—numbers that embody all of the choices, events, and happenstances of the research that will be formally admitted as evidence in the scientific court within which we are trying to judge treatment effectiveness. These numbers carry the information about measured differences between the experimental groups that is crucial to judging treatment effects. They also reflect whatever variability has been introduced to the research through sampling error, subject heterogeneity, procedural inconsistency, measurement unreliability, and the like. Additionally, they include whatever information is available for formal consideration regarding the implementation of treatment, characteristics of subjects, timing of measurement, and other such important contextual features of the research.

The crucial part of the data analysis in treatment effectiveness research is the testing of statistical significance for the difference between treatment and control groups on each dependent measure of interest. If a difference is statistically significant it constitutes a "finding" which is the centerpiece of the evidence that the treatment had an effect. Conversely, if that difference is not statistically significant, the case for a treatment effect is seriously weakened.

Statistical power in this context is the probability that statistical significance will be attained *given* that there really is a treatment effect. Earlier, we described a sensitive research design as one capable of detecting a treatment effect of meaningful magnitude. Since, in conventional practice, detecting a treatment effect means finding a statistically significant difference between the treatment and control group scores, design sensitivity can be expressed in terms of its consequences for statistical power. A sensitive design is one yielding data for which the central test of statistical significance has high statistical power. That is, if the treatment did in fact have an effect, the treatment versus control group difference will most likely be statistically significant.

Chapter 2 discusses the statistical power framework in more detail, and additional elaboration is presented in Chapters 3 and 4. For these introductory remarks, however, we now turn our attention to the reasons why design sensitivity and, more specifically, statistical power deserve much more attention in treatment effectiveness research than they typically receive.

The Neglect of Statistical Power

Experimental designs that lack sensitivity and, correspondingly, statistical comparisons that lack power make for treatment effectiveness research that cannot accomplish its central purpose—to determine the effects of treatment. It would be comforting to have some assurance that typical research practices in the behavioral sciences ensured adequate statistical power. Unfortunately, no such comfort can be provided. What evidence we have on this matter indicates just the contrary—that statistical power is generally shamefully low.

A number of reviewers, for instance, have made collections of research studies in different areas of inquiry and assessed the statistical power of the significance tests reported there. The customary procedure is to identify the order of magnitude of effects considered "small," "medium," and "large" in the domain of interest, then determine the average power of the studies actually conducted in that domain for detecting such effects.

Small, medium, and large effects in this context are most frequently defined according to the rules of thumb proposed by Cohen in his book, *Statistical Power Analysis for the Behavioral Sciences* (1977, 1988), which has become the standard reference on statistical power in the social sciences. Cohen represented the effect size on some dependent measure used in an experiment in terms of the difference between the treatment and control group means expressed in standard deviation units (σ). This way of indexing effect size will receive more detailed discussion in Chapters 2 and 3. For now, it is sufficient to recognize that the spread of scores for most measures on most populations or samples in the behavioral sciences is about five standard deviations from the lowest value to the highest (because of the ubiquity of the normal curve for such scores). This relative uniformity makes it meaningful to express the difference between a treatment group mean and a control group mean in standard deviation units irrespective of the particular measure used. Cohen reported that across a wide sampling of behavioral science research, effects of around .8σ were at the large end of the range of what has been found, .5σ was about medium, and .2σ was at the small end of the range.

With these rules of thumb for effect size, we can examine the statistical power in the various research domains investigated by the reviewers mentioned earlier. Their findings are summarized in Table 1.1 which shows the average statistical power (which, recall, is the probability of attaining statistical significance) found in each research domain for detecting effects of different size.

Note that Table 1.1 does not tell us what size effects are actually present in these various research domains. What it tells us about is the statistical power of the significance tests typically used in those domains. For example, the average power of the tests of treatment effects in evaluation research for detecting small effects is .28. That is, if a small effect were in fact present, the typical test would yield statistical significance only 28% of the time and yield null results (nonsignificance) 72% of the time. We do not know if small effects are really present, only that the research is not very likely to detect them if they are.

While the procedural differences in the reviews summarized in Table 1.1 make it difficult to compare them with each other, the striking thing about the overall results is the low level of statistical power represented in almost all cases. We presume that researchers would want to design research that has a high probability of detecting any nontrivial effects that occur. A power of .90 or .95 might be quite reasonable in many research contexts; Cohen (1977, 1988) recommended .80 as a minimal standard. As Table 1.1 demonstrates, however, the typical research design in most of these areas attained the .80 level of statistical power, if at all, only for large effects. Moreover, many of the reviews represented in Table 1.1 included correlational and survey research, both of which typically use larger samples than does experimental research. Thus these figures, low as they are, probably overestimate the statistical power for the subsets of treatment effectiveness research contained within them.

The conclusion to be drawn here is that most research studies in the social sciences are woefully underpowered for reliably detecting anything but large effects. If effects in the small or medium range do in fact occur in this research, high proportions of the studies will nonetheless produce null results. It is possible, of course, that treatment effects in the small and even the medium range are so small as to have no practical significance and hence not be worth detecting. Table 1.1 can be interpreted as an indication

TABLE 1.1 Reviews of Statistical Power Levels in Various Research Domains

	Average statistical power reported for detecting:		
Research domain	"Small" effects	"Medium" effects	"Large" effects
Evaluation research	.28	.63	.81
Applied psychology	.25	.67	.86
Social psychology	.18	.48	.83
Sociology	.55	.84	.94
Education (a)	.13	.47	.73
Mathematics education	.24	.62	.83
Mass communication	.34	.76	.91
Management research	.31	.77	.91
Marketing research (b)	.24	.69	.87
Communication	.18	.52	.79
Speech pathology	.16	.44	.73
Occupational therapy (c)	.37	.65	.93
Gerontology	.37	.88	.96
Medicine	.14	.39	.61

NOTE: (a) Included only F- and t-tests yielding statistical significance
(b) Experimental studies only
(c) Power in each category only for studies with computed effect sizes in the indicated range
SOURCES (respectively): Lipsey et al., 1985; Chase and Chase, 1976; Cohen, 1962; Spreitzer, 1974 (cited in Chase and Tucker, 1976); Brewer, 1972; Clark, 1974 (cited in Reed and Slaichert, 1981); Chase and Baran, 1976; Mazen, Graf, Kellogg, and Hemmasi, 1987; Sawyer and Ball, 1981; Chase and Tucker, 1975; Kroll and Chase, 1975; Ottenbacher, 1982; Levenson, 1980; Reed and Slaichert, 1981

that most researchers in the behavioral sciences deliberately design their studies to detect only large effects and screen out smaller effects as negligible. Perhaps researchers correctly perceive that effects in this range are trivial.

As will be made more evident in subsequent chapters of this volume, the position that treatment effects in Cohen's small and medium ranges are universally of negligible practical significance is difficult to sustain. To begin with, such effects are as much a function of the characteristics of the research design and procedures as of the impact of treatment and therefore may be poor indicators of the latter (see Chapters 3–7). Moreover, the effects actually obtained in a wide range of treatment effectiveness research in fact fall in Cohen's small to medium range (see Chapter 3). If this range is trivial then we must conclude that a high proportion of treatments in behavioral science lacks meaningful practical significance, a discomforting conclusion. Conversely, certain effects of rather clear practical significance, such as one grade level of reading ability for elementary and high school students (Carver, 1975) or differences in batting skill among professional baseball players (Abelson, 1985), often manifest themselves as small statistical effects on credible performance measures.

Most persuasive, perhaps, is the simple translation of the rather abstract statistical effect-size indicator of standard deviation units into terms more easily grasped. Such translation will be considered more fully in Chapter 3, but one example now will serve to illustrate the rather different impression of practical significance this procedure can produce. Cohen's small effect does indeed sound trivial when described as two-tenths of a standard deviation. Rosenthal and Rubin (1982), on the other hand, have converted this statistical index into simple success rates, that is, the proportions of treatment and control groups respectively that exceed the overall median outcome score. When viewed this way, a treatment effect of two-tenths of a standard deviation corresponds to a difference of about 10 percentage points between the treatment group success rate and the control group success rate.

Suppose, for instance, that in a control group of cancer patients receiving conventional therapy, 55 of 100 die within one year. An experimental treatment that produced a $.2\sigma$ better result would reduce the death rate to 45 per 100, a savings of 10 lives. Put another way, with a treatment effect of this "small" order of magnitude, 18% fewer people die than would have without treatment (10/55). When statistical effects are interpreted in this manner, it is difficult to argue that $.2\sigma$ is necessarily a trivial effect.

We might grant, therefore, that a small effect of $.2\sigma$ could be meaningful in treatment effectiveness research. But we still do not know whether effects that large do, in fact, occur frequently in such research. If behavioral science treatments are generally ineffective, the typical research study will mostly produce the right conclusion (nonsignificance) irrespective of its statistical power—high powered research cannot detect what is not there and low powered research cannot detect much of anything. To assess more definitively the extent to which low statistical power is a problem for treatment effectiveness research, therefore, what we really want is to compare the statistical conclusions of typical treatment versus control group significance testing with the "true" state of affairs regarding the effects of the treatment under investigation. Knowing the true effects, however, is a tall order.

One approach is to turn to meta-analysis for a better estimate of "true" treatment effects or, at least, for an estimate of treatment effects with assured statistical power. Meta-analysis is a technique for statistically aggregating the results of a number of individual research studies by pooling the effect size estimates from each (Glass, McGaw, & Smith, 1981; Rosenthal, 1984). In their meta-analysis of psychotherapy treatment effectiveness research, for example, Smith and Glass (1977) computed 833 effect sizes from the sample values found in 375 studies of psychotherapy treatment. The grand mean effect size over all those studies was .68σ and represented research on approximately 25,000 subjects. We can think of the grand mean effect size for meta-analysis as a kind of main effect of the treatment of interest averaged over the wide variety of treatment and subject variations, research circumstances, measures, and so forth represented in the set of research studies included in the meta-analysis.

If we take the grand mean effect size from meta-analysis of research in a particular treatment domain as a better estimate of the "true" effect size than that produced by any one study in that domain, we have some basis for judging the range of effects that might actually be produced by the treatments of interest in such research. Since dozens of treatment effectiveness meta-analyses have been conducted in the last decade, there is sufficient depth in the literature to make a useful analysis. The author's current collection of such meta-analyses numbers 186 and covers more than 100 different types of treatment or intervention in the areas of mental health, health, education, and work. Among the treatments represented, for instance, are psychotherapy, programmed learning, job enrichment, and pregnancy education.

More details about these meta-analyses are presented in Chapter 3. For present purposes, it is sufficient to note that they reported 229 grand mean effect sizes which summarized the results of about 10,000 individual treatment effectiveness studies. Of those grand mean effect sizes, 77% were .2σ or greater—that is, at least as large as Cohen's rule of thumb for a small effect. Moreover, 36% of them were .5σ or greater (i.e., at least medium) and 12% were .8σ or greater (large). Though meta-analysis is by no means a perfect indicator of the magnitude of the "true" effect sizes produced by treatment, these figures nonetheless make it quite implausible that the great majority of such treatments have trivial or null effects. We cannot assume, therefore, that null results from low powered research are often correct "by accident" because the treatments under study were generally ineffective anyway.

For 44 of the meta-analyses in this collection, an even closer examination can be made of the extent to which the statistical significance testing done at the individual study level accurately reflected the treatment effects found at the meta-analysis level. These 44 meta-analyses reported specifically on the statistical significance found in the individual studies aggregated in the meta-analysis. Note first that of the grand mean effect sizes reported in these meta-analyses, 37 were $.2\sigma$ or larger (averaging $.49\sigma$). Such results suggest that the treatment effects actually present were at least small by Cohen's guidelines and centered in the medium range. Despite the apparent treatment effects in these 37 treatment domains, only 45% of the 2394 tests of the statistical significance of treatment-control differences conducted in the individual studies represented in these meta-analyses were significant. Put the other way around, even though there were apparently real treatment effects present in these cases, 55% of the significance tests gave null results.

This last result is worth emphasizing. It means that a researcher conducting treatment effectiveness research on genuinely effective treatments may have more than a 50% chance of coming to the *wrong* statistical conclusion. This is a shockingly high error rate. It means that the same accuracy would be produced if the research effort were abandoned and, instead, the researcher simply flipped a coin, announcing statistical significance for heads and nonsignificance for tails. Even more accurate (if these meta-analyses are correct in indicating that, overall, nearly 80% of the treatments represented have at least small effects) would be to simply announce statistical significance in every case irrespective of the results of the research. Clearly, if individual treatment effectiveness studies are to be correct in their statistical conclusions, researchers must give much greater attention to the sensitivity of their designs.

Conclusions

Error in statistical significance testing is widespread in treatment effectiveness research and, correspondingly, the accuracy of the conclusions drawn from these tests is low. Such spurious overacceptance of the null hypothesis has very undesirable consequences for our understanding of the effects of treatment. For example, low statistical power can easily produce a majority of null results in a research area where, in fact, the treatments are universally effective. Such high proportions of null results are generally interpreted as a failure of the treatment to show meaningful or consistent effects. Unless statistical power is kept high, however, such results are more accurately described as a failure of the research methods to detect the effects, not a failure of the treatment to produce effects. The resulting confusion and inconsistency in the research literature confound our ability to draw meaningful conclusions. As a result, many treatment areas are marked by a history of successive literature reviews reporting ambiguity or outright negative conclusions about the efficacy of the treatment (Fischer, 1978; Prather & Gibson, 1977; Rossi & Wright, 1984).

One can easily conclude from a broad review of such research that "nothing works." This pessimistic conclusion undermines our faith in our social efficacy—our ability to undertake deliberate intervention in undesirable social circumstances and make them better. It exacerbates the natural tension between practitioners, convinced on the basis of experience that their ministrations are beneficial to the recipients, and researchers, who never seem to be able to turn up positive results when they study those efforts. And, perhaps most important, this state of affairs degrades our ability to learn from research: to differentiate successful treatments from unsuccessful ones and find the keys to making the successful ones work even better.

It is the premise of this book that a primary obligation of the researcher studying treatment effectiveness is to ensure that adequate statistical power will be attained in the final data analysis. Statistical power should be the foundation upon which the design is constructed and the base upon which efforts to ensure internal, construct, and external validity rest. Since the degree of statistical power depends on a complex series of decisions the researcher makes about the plan, implementation, and statistical analysis for the research, it is something that must be designed into a study from the very beginning. The remainder of this volume is devoted to further exploration of the concept of statistical power and, especially, to examining a variety of practical approaches and techniques a researcher can use to enhance the sensitivity of treatment effectiveness research design so that it attains adequate power.

2. The Statistical Power Framework

Statistical power is the probability that a statistical test of the null hypothesis upon sample data will (correctly) yield statistical significance when the null hypothesis is, in fact, false for the population from which the sample is drawn. In treatment effectiveness research, interest centers on the difference between treatment and control groups on the mean value of an outcome measure of interest. The null hypothesis is that treatment and control group scores are drawn from the same population. That is, there is no "real" difference between them, and any observed difference only reflects sampling error. Rejecting the null hypothesis (finding statistical significance) indicates that the observed difference is larger than is likely from sampling error alone, making it improbable that treatment and control populations are really the same.

Note that it is *not* a matter of probability whether the population means for the various experimental conditions actually differ. Either they do or they do not and if we knew the population scores we could determine the differences between the means directly without any statistical test. When we employ statistical inference in treatment effectiveness research, therefore, it is always under one of two circumstances:

1) The population means for different experimental conditions really do not differ; that is, the experimental conditions have no differential effect. In this case, the null hypothesis is true and the correct finding is to fail to reject it, that is, fail to attain significance in the statistical test. The only error in the statistical conclusions that can be made in these circumstances is to attain statistical significance falsely, a mistake known as Type I or alpha (α) error. Conventional statistical analysis estimates the probability of making this error directly by assuming the null hypothesis and calculating the likelihood of the obtained results. By custom we usually accept no more than an estimated 5% probability of making a Type I error ($\alpha = .05$). Conversely, if the statistical conclusion is not in error it must be correct, and the probability of that is $1 - \alpha$ or .95 when α is set at .05.

2) The population means for different experimental conditions really do differ; that is, there is a "true" effect. In this case, the null hypothesis is false and the correct finding is to reject it, that is, attain significance in the statistical test. The only error in the statistical conclusions that can be made in these circumstances is to fail to attain statistical significance, a mistake called Type II or beta (β) error. Since conventional statistical analysis assumes the null hypothesis, it does not provide a direct estimate of the probability of making this error. In order to obtain such an estimate, we must first assume that the population means do in fact differ by a specified magnitude (represented as the "decentrality parameter" or "effect size" in statistical power analysis). We must then estimate the probability that differences among the sample means will nonetheless fall (by chance) within the nonsignificant range produced by the null hypothesis model. That probability, β, represents the likelihood of Type II error. Conversely, 1-β represents the probability of a correct conclusion, that is, statistical significance rather than nonsignificance. As the probability of finding significance when the null hypothesis is in fact false, 1-β is statistical power. There are no widely accepted conventions for permissible levels of Type II error in statistical analysis nor for the minimal level of statistical power.

For the prototypical case of treatment effectiveness research where interest centers on the mean difference between treatment group scores and control group scores, therefore, there are four possible scenarios for the outcome of statistical significance testing. There either is or is not a real (population) treatment versus control difference and, for each case, the statistical test either is or is not significant. The various combinations can be depicted in a 2 × 2 table along with the associated probabilities as shown in Table 2.1.

Note that α and β in Table 2.1 are statements of *conditional* probabilities. That is, they are of the form: *if* the null hypothesis is true [false], *then* the probability of an erroneous statistical conclusion is α [β]. It follows that the total probability of error in an experimental study is *either* α or β, not both or some combination of the two and certainly not always α. Thus when the null hypothesis is true, the probability of a statistical conclusion error is held to 5% by the convention of α = .05. When the null hypothesis is false, however, the probability of error is β, and β can be quite large (and often is, as shown in Chapter 1). Many researchers may be surprised to learn that the probability of an erroneous conclusion in a statistical analysis is not necessarily limited to .05 but may easily range as high as .85 or more.

TABLE 2.1 The Possibilities of Error in Statistical Significance Testing of
Treatment (T) versus Control (C) Group Differences

	Population circumstances	
Conclusion from statistical test on sample data	T and C differ	T and C do not differ
Significant difference (reject null hypothesis)	Correct conclusion Probability = $1-\beta$ (power)	Type I error Probability = α
No significant difference (fail to reject null hypothesis)	Type II error Probability = β	Correct conclusion Probability = $1-\alpha$

The null hypothesis, of course, is usually adopted only for statistical purposes by researchers who believe it to be false and expect to reject it. We therefore often have the curious situation of researchers who assume that the probability of error that applies to their research is β (that is, they assume the null hypothesis is false), yet permit β to be so high that they have more chance of being wrong than right when they interpret the statistical significance of their results. While such behavior is not altogether rational, it is perhaps understandable given the minuscule emphasis placed on Type II error and statistical power in the teaching and practice of statistical analysis and design in the behavioral sciences.

The Elements of Statistical Power

There are four factors that determine statistical power. We first list them in summary form, then discuss in more detail the special problems each poses for treatment effectiveness research.

Statistical test. Since determination of statistical significance and estimation of the probability of error in the statistical conclusion are made within the framework of a particular statistical test, the test itself is one of the factors determining statistical power. Statistical tests are such procedures as the *t*-test, F-test, Chi-square, and so forth that are appropriate for various circumstances of statistical significance testing depending upon the assumptions made about the structure of the data, the sampling and populations, the nature of the difference or relationship being tested, and other such matters. Different statistical tests do not necessarily have the same statistical power when they are applied to the same data.

Alpha level. The level set for alpha influences the likelihood of statistical significance—larger alpha makes significance easier to attain than smaller alpha. The likelihood of significance in cases where the null hypothesis is false, that is, power, will therefore increase as alpha is increased.

Sample size. Statistical significance testing is concerned with sampling error, the expectable discrepancies between sample values and the corresponding population value for a given statistic (such as a difference between means). Since sampling error is greater for small samples and almost negligible for very large samples, it follows that sample size is a major determinant of the probability of errors in statistical conclusions and thus of statistical power.

Effect size. If the null hypothesis is false, then there is some real difference between the experimental conditions. The size of this difference, or effect, will have an important influence on the likelihood of attaining statistical significance. The larger the effect, the more probable is statistical significance and the greater the statistical power.

For a given dependent measure in treatment effectiveness research, effect size can be thought of as the difference between the means for the treatment versus control populations or, for more than two groups, as the variance among the population means ("between-groups" variance). In this form, however, effect size is partly a matter of how the dependent measure is scaled. For example, a given difference between two populations might be 20 points on a measure ranging from 0 to 100 but only 2 points if each score is arbitrarily divided by 10 to make a scale ranging from 0 to 10. With an effect size formulation tied so closely to the features of a specific scale of measurement, it is difficult to make general statements about statistical power.

For most purposes, therefore, it is preferable to use an effect size formulation (or index) that somehow "standardizes" differences between means to adjust for arbitrary units of measurement. In behavioral science statistics such standardization is typically accomplished by dividing the scores by the standard deviation of their distribution to produce a measure in standard deviation units rather than in the units of the original scale. The effect size for a given difference between means, therefore, can be represented as follows:

$$ES = \frac{\mu_t - \mu_c}{\sigma}$$

Where μ_t and μ_c are the respective means for the treatment and control populations and σ is their common standard deviation ($\sigma = \sigma_t = \sigma_c$).

Depicted graphically in Figure 2.1, the effect size is the ratio of the size of the difference between means marked Δ to the common standard deviation marked σ.

As noted in Chapter 1, ES is the effect size index popularized by Cohen (1977, 1988) for purposes of statistical power analysis and widely adopted (with variation) in meta-analysis to represent the magnitude of treatment effects (e.g., Glass, McGaw, & Smith, 1981; Hedges & Olkin, 1985; Rosenthal, 1984).

It is worth emphasizing that for statistical power analysis effect size is a *population* parameter—it is defined in terms of the relevant population means and standard deviations. Like other population parameters, it generally cannot be determined directly; when values are needed, they are estimated from sample data.

Variations on the effect size index for situations other than simple two-group comparisons and differences between means are presented in Chapter 4. For now, we will use ES as a generic index of effect size in treatment effectiveness research. Note again that this formulation is general for all dependent variables—it expresses the effect in standard deviation units, not in the units of the particular measure used. Thus the outcome variable might be an attitude measure, an achievement test, a count of speech errors, or whatever. In each case, the effect size index reports that the treatment group mean is so many standard deviations larger (or smaller) than the control group mean. By convention, we compute ES so that positive values indicate a "better" outcome for the treatment group than for the control group and negative values indicate a "better" outcome for the control group.

An Example

If we focus on statistical significance testing in treatment effectiveness research, the most common circumstances is an analysis that compares the mean score on a dependent measure for a treatment group with the mean

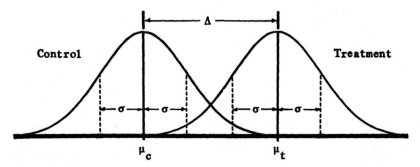

Figure 2.1: Graphical Depiction of the Effect Size for Comparison of the Distribution of Scores for a Treatment Group and a Control Group

score for a control group. Since statistical power has to do with the probability of attaining statistical significance, we will consider step-by-step the factors that influence whether significance is found in this simple comparison.

Note first that the analysis can be made using various statistical tests, for example, t-test, one-way analysis of variance, Chi-square, Mann-Whitney U test, and so forth. Some of these are algebraically equivalent (e.g., t-test and one-way ANOVA), others are not (e.g., t-test and Mann-Whitney U test). Those that are not equivalent will not necessarily agree with regard to the statistical significance of any difference between the treatment and control group means. The choice of a statistical test will therefore be one factor affecting the statistical conclusion.

Suppose we choose the t-test for this particular analysis. Computationally, we construct a ratio using the familiar formula below:

$$t = \frac{\bar{X}_t - \bar{X}_c}{s\sqrt{1/n_t + 1/n_c}}$$

Where $\bar{X}_t$ and $\bar{X}_c$ are the sample means for the treatment and control groups respectively, n_t and n_c are the sample sizes for those groups, and s is the pooled within samples standard deviation used to estimate the population standard deviation.

If this t-ratio is sufficiently large, larger than a specific "critical value" looked up in a table of such values, we will declare the treatment versus control group difference statistically significant. The critical value with which we compare the computed t is a function of the selected alpha level, the directionality of the null hypothesis, and the degrees of freedom (n_t + n_c − 2 for the t-test). The larger the alpha value selected, for example, .10 rather than .05, the smaller the critical value needed for statistical significance and the easier significance is to attain. Moreover, for a given alpha level, a directional or one-tailed test of a difference only in favor of the treatment group will yield significance at smaller critical values than a non-directional or two-tailed test of a difference favoring either group. Thus alpha and the direction of differences tested are factors in determining the likelihood of statistical significance. So, too, is the sample size since larger samples yield larger degrees of freedom which, in turn, have somewhat smaller critical values for attaining significance. The more important role of sample size, however, comes within the computed t-ratio itself.

The computed t-ratio, like any ratio, will be large, and hence more likely to be significant, when the numerator is "large" or when the denominator is "small." The numerator of the t-ratio is the difference between the treatment group mean and the control group mean, that is, the "unstandardized" effect size. The denominator of the t-ratio is the standard error of the difference of the means and represents an estimate of the variance that can be expected in the differences between the means of pairs of samples drawn from the single parent population assumed under the null hypothesis.

If we use $ES' = (\bar{X}_t - \bar{X}_c)/s$ to represent the effect size as estimated from sample data, the t-ratio thus can be expressed in terms of ES' as follows:

$$ t = \frac{(\bar{X}_t - \bar{X}_c)/s}{\sqrt{1/n_t + 1/n_c}} = \frac{ES'}{\sqrt{1/n_t + 1/n_c}} $$

In this formulation we can identify an estimate of the population effect size ES (designated ES') in the same standardized form in which it was discussed earlier, that is, the difference between the means of two distributions divided by their common standard deviation. As ES increases, the t-ratio and the likelihood of statistical significance increase as well.

The second term in this formulation, $\sqrt{1/n_t + 1/n_c}$, isolates the influence of sample size on the magnitude of the t-ratio. As the n's in this expression get larger, the value of the expression itself gets smaller. Since this expression is in the denominator of the t-ratio, smaller values make t larger. Thus we see directly how larger sample sizes increase the likelihood of statistical significance for a given effect size.

Though this example is presented in terms of the t-test, the same pattern of relationships holds for virtually all the familiar test statistics. In each case, with some variations, the test statistic can be factored into a component reflecting the effect size in standardized form and a component reflecting sample size (Cohen, 1970). The critical value to which the test statistic is compared for assessing statistical significance, in turn, is a function of alpha and a degrees-of-freedom term that is itself based primarily on sample size.

From this example, therefore, we see once again that the factors that enter into the determination of statistical significance, and hence statistical power, are the statistical test, the alpha level, the sample size, and the effect size. The most complex of these terms is the effect size, and it will require considerable discussion in the next chapter and later in this volume. For now, however, we want to review the four factors of statistical power in the context of treatment effectiveness research to highlight the special difficulties that can be presented by each.

Statistical Test

Most typically, treatment effectiveness research designs are simple group comparisons, one treatment group compared with one control group or, perhaps, a few treatment variations compared with one or more control groups. The statistical tests for analyzing such designs are among the most familiar—t-test, one-way analysis of variance, Chi-square, and so forth. These tests use an "error term" based on the within-groups variability in the sample data to assess the likelihood that a mean difference between the groups would result from sampling error. If the variability on the scores for dependent measures within the treatment and control groups is very large, it makes statistical significance for a given mean difference between the groups more difficult to attain and lowers the statistical power of the test.

Unfortunately for statistical power, there are many features distinctive to treatment effectiveness research that can cause the within-group variability in sample data to be large. For instance, practical treatment effectiveness research generally samples from "real world" populations of potential beneficiaries that can be quite heterogeneous in comparison, say, to the college students favored in much behavioral science research. Similarly, the measures used in practical research may depend upon clinical records, unsystematic observations, and innovative approaches that have lower than optimal reliability. Moreover, such research must often be conducted in the field rather than in the laboratory, allowing for additional variability stemming from inconsistent measurement procedures, variations in treatment implementation and dosage, and the like.

To the extent that within-group variability can be eliminated, minimized, or somehow offset, treatment effectiveness research will be more powerful, that is, more sensitive to true treatment effects if they are present. Much of what is at issue here has to do with the effect size parameter in statistical power which is, after all, a direct reflection of between-group differences in relation to within-group variability. The procedure selected for statistical significance testing, however, plays an important role. That test reflects certain assumptions about the sampling, the nature of the data, and the circumstances in which the null hypothesis should be rejected that bear importantly on the likelihood of statistical significance, especially in situations of relatively high variability on the dependent measure.

Three aspects of the statistical test are paramount in this regard. First, for a given set of treatment versus control group data, different tests may have different formulations of the sampling error estimate and the critical test values needed for significance. They may, therefore, differ in whether they attain significance for a given set of data, a difference in the inherent power of the test. Nonparametric tests, those that use only rank order or categorical (yes/no; high/low) information from dependent variable scores, generally have less inherent power than do parametric tests, those that use scores representing degrees of the variable along some continuum. Issues involved in this choice are further discussed in Chapter 4.

Second, a given statistical test can be used with a null hypothesis of "no difference" between groups in either direction (nondirectional or two-tailed test) or with a null hypothesis specifying "no difference" between groups in only one direction (directional or one-tailed test). A nondirectional test means we reject the null hypothesis if either treatment or control is superior to the other; a directional test means we specify which is expected to be superior and test only for that difference. In comparing weight loss on a multivitamin diet to a placebo control, for example, a nondirectional statistical test would examine both the possibility that the weight loss for the diet group was significantly greater than that for the control group and the possibility that it was significantly smaller. A directional test, on the other hand, would test only results in the "expected" direction, that is, whether weight loss was greater for the diet group. Though they are of more limited scope, directional tests have greater statistical power (all other things being equal) than have nondirectional tests.

The third aspect of a statistical test that is relevant to its power concerns the way it partitions sampling error and which components of that error variance are used in the significance test. It is often the case in treatment effectiveness research that a certain amount of the variability on a given dependent measure is associated with subject characteristics that are not likely to change as a result of treatment. If certain factors extraneous to the treatment issues contribute substantially to the population variability on the dependent measure of interest, the variability resulting from those factors can be removed from the estimate of sampling error against which differences between treatment and control groups are tested. By making the "denominator" terms smaller in such a test, the test ratio for a given group difference (numerator) will be larger, statistical significance will be more easily attained, and statistical power will be greater.

Partitioning the error variance in a statistical test requires a procedure that makes use of information about those extraneous variables with which the dependent measures are correlated. Such procedures include blocking (in analysis of variance) and analysis of covariance to control variability associated with subject characteristics other than the dependent variable. They also include the correlated t-test and repeated measures or split-plot analysis of variance designs that control that variability among subjects stemming from different individual baselines (pretreatment starting point) on the dependent measure itself. In either case, these tests assume a sampling procedure that draws subjects from groups that are relatively homogeneous on the variable being controlled and that estimates the corresponding sampling error accordingly.

These variations on sampling assumptions and statistical test procedures will be more fully explored in Chapters 4 and 6. For now, a simple example might best illustrate the issues. Suppose that men and women differ greatly on some measure, for example, the amount of weight they can lift. Suppose further that we wanted to assess the effects of an exercise treatment that was expected to increase muscular strength. Forming treatment and control groups by simple random sampling of the undifferentiated population would mean that part of the "luck of the draw," that is, the sampling error, would be the chance proportions of men versus women that end up in each experimental group and, additionally, would mean that part of the population variability would be the natural differences between men and women. This source of variability may well be judged irrelevant to assessing the treatment effect—treatment may rightfully be judged effective if it increases the strength of women relative to the natural variability in women's strength and that of men relative to the natural variability in men's strength. The corresponding sampling procedure is not simple random sampling but stratified random sampling, drawing women and men separately from their respective populations. The corresponding statistical test is the blocked analysis of variance (ANOVA) which analyzes differences between experimental conditions in relation to the variability within, not between, the male and female blocks.

The challenge to the treatment effectiveness researcher on this issue, therefore, is to identify, insofar as possible, the measurable extraneous factors that contribute to population variability and use a sampling strategy and corresponding statistical test that assesses treatment effects against an appropriate estimate of sampling error. In cases of few or no factors extraneous to the treatment issues contributing to population variability on the dependent measure of interest, simple group comparison tests are quite adequate—t-test, one-way ANOVA, and so forth. However, where there are important extraneous factors (and there almost always are), failing to use a statistical test that accounts for them can greatly reduce the ability of the research to detect real treatment effects.

Alpha Level

Alpha is conventionally set at .05 for statistical significance testing and, on the surface, may seem to be the one straightforward and unproblematic element of statistical power for the treatment effectiveness researcher. That impression, however, is quite misleading. An alpha of .05 corresponds to a .95 probability of a correct statistical conclusion when the null hypothesis is true $(1 - \alpha)$. As shown in Chapter 1, power $(1 - \beta)$, the analogous probability of a correct statistical conclusion when the null hypothesis is false, rarely attains a level as high as .95 for any but the largest effects. By making statistical significance harder to attain and, therefore, power lower, a relatively conservative alpha can make a bad situation worse. We must ask if it makes sense to have a high level of protection against Type I error and little protection against Type II error. Such a posture would be reasonable only if a persuasive case could be made that the implications of Type I error in the research were very much more serious than those of Type II error.

For *basic* research in the behavioral sciences, such a case might generally be made. The nature of basic research is such that the researcher should rightfully be very conservative about accepting new facts from experiment. Claiming that there is a relationship or an effect when, in fact, there is none (Type I error) can mislead investigators about the evidence to be accounted for and seriously hamper theory development. Finding no relationship when, in fact, there is one (Type II error), on the other hand, generally has less serious consequences. A null finding does not easily become definitive in basic research nor is it typically the basis for theoretical advance. In basic research, therefore, it is usually desirable to keep the probability of Type I error low even at the expense of accepting an increased likelihood of Type II error.

Treatment effectiveness research, however, is often applied research.

For example, a promising treatment might be investigated to determine if it has beneficial effects in some problem area. In such applied research the implications of errors of inference may be quite different from those in basic research. To "discover" that an applied treatment is effective when, in fact, it is not, does indeed mislead practitioners just as the analogous case misleads theoreticians. Practitioners, however, are often in situations where they must act as effectively as they can irrespective of the state of their formal knowledge, and it is not unusual for them to use treatments and techniques of plausible but unproven efficacy. Moreover, demonstrably effective treatments for many practical problems are not easy to come by and candidates should not be too easily dismissed. Accepting a relatively high probability of Type I error in applied treatment effectiveness research amounts to giving a treatment the benefit of the doubt about whether statistically modest effects represent treatment efficacy or merely sampling error.

A high probability of Type II error, however, presents a rather different circumstance. In that case the research is likely to yield null results for a genuinely effective treatment. Not surprisingly, such results are often taken to indicate that the treatment does not work. In a context where effective treatment is needed and not readily available, a Type II error can represent a great practical loss—an effective treatment is falsely discredited. In applied treatment effectiveness research it may often be desirable to keep the likelihood of such error low even at the expense of accepting an increased probability of Type I error.

In a broader view, what is being discussed here is a kind of cost-risk analysis. For the basic researcher, at least in the behavioral sciences, hypotheses are usually cheap—with a little time and a good armchair, dozens can be generated. The challenge is to identify the valid ones, and the researcher does not want to accept much risk of claiming that one is valid when it is not. For the practitioner or applied researcher, on the other hand, hypotheses are not necessarily cheap. Good ideas about how to approach a problem effectively are hard to come by and are often difficult and expensive to work out in sufficient operational detail to be properly investigated. The more serious risk in this case may be that of testing a genuinely effective treatment and failing to recognize its efficacy.

The global categories of basic and applied research, of course, are of limited value when it is time to design a study. More appropriate is explicit consideration of the cost-risk issues as they apply to the particular circumstances at hand. At the first level of analysis, the researcher might compare the relative seriousness of Type I and Type II errors. The specific issues that determine the seriousness of the respective errors will be distinctive to each study. If they were judged as equally serious, the risk of each should be kept comparable, that is, alpha should equal beta. Alternatively, if one were judged as more serious than the other, it should be held to a stricter standard even at the expense of relaxing the other. This kind of analysis would permit the limits of acceptable risk for Type I and Type II error to be set quite explicitly in terms of their consequences. Chapter 6 discusses this approach to setting alpha in treatment effectiveness research.

More common than a reasoned approach, unfortunately, is reliance on convention, and alpha is almost universally set at .05. There is no corresponding convention for beta (probability of Type II error), which may be one of the reasons it is so widely neglected in behavioral science research. Cohen (1977, 1988) suggested $\beta = .20$ as a reasonable value for general use or, more specifically, he suggested .80 as a desirable minimum for statistical power $(1 - \beta)$. This suggestion represents a judgment that Type I error is four times as serious as Type II error, a position that may be more in line with the concerns of basic research than of applied research.

Sample Size

The relationship between sample size and statistical power is so close that most textbooks that discuss power at all do so in terms of determining the sample size necessary to attain a desired power level. In some ways this emphasis is unfortunate because it leaves the impression that statistical power is solely a matter of sample size and, correspondingly, that increasing sample size is the only way to increase power. While enlarging sample size is an important and very useful way to raise statistical power, sample size is only one of the four factors that determine power. In many cases adjustment to one or more of the other factors may have a more beneficial effect on power than would any attainable increase in sample size.

It is worth digressing a moment to clarify what is being counted when we talk about sample size or number of subjects, since there is occasional confusion on this point in the treatment effectiveness literature. What is important here is to recognize that a sampling unit is a concept of statistics and not a concept about people or other entities that might be involved in the research. The statistical sampling unit in experimental research is the one that is independently drawn from a population and assigned to an experimental condition. Thus if individual persons are selected and assigned, as is often the case in such research, the sampling unit is one person and the sample size is the number of persons assigned to each condition. If, however, selection and assignment are made using some larger unit, then it is that unit which should be counted irrespective of how many persons may be within it. For example, if whole classrooms are selected and assigned to different experimental conditions, the sampling unit is the classroom and the sample size is the number of classrooms, not the number of students in the classrooms. Statistical analysis using number of students as the sample size is fallacious in such a case and, in particular, gives a very misleading impression of statistical power by presuming larger samples than are actually involved.

The difficulty that the relationship between sample size and statistical power poses for practical research, especially treatment effectiveness research, is that the availability of subjects is often quite limited. While one can increase power considerably by parading a larger number of subjects through the study, there have to be subjects ready to march before this becomes a practical strategy. In circumstances with real clients for real treatments there may be relatively few persons appropriate for the treatment. Or, if there are enough appropriate persons, there may be limits on the facilities for treating them or, if facilities are adequate, few who will volunteer or whom program personnel are willing to assign or, if assigned, few who will sustain their participation until the study is complete.

A related factor is the cost of adding subjects to a research study. The number of subjects that must be recruited, assigned to experimental conditions, treated, monitored, and measured is a major determinant of the cost of treatment effectiveness research. Additionally, in many fields of research it is necessary to pay subjects for their participation, further adding to the expense. Under such circumstances, even when subjects are available, it may not be economically feasible to design research with very large samples. The challenge for the treatment effectiveness researcher, therefore, is often one of keeping power at an adequate level with quite modest sample sizes.

If modest sample sizes generally provided adequate power, this particular challenge would not be very demanding. Unfortunately, they do not. Indeed, the sample sizes needed to increase the statistical power of typical treatment effectiveness research to adequate levels are considerably larger than in conventional practice. For example, the mean sample size found by Lipsey, Crosse, Dunkle, Pollard, and Stobart (1985) in a collection of published treatment effectiveness studies was about 40, that is, an average of 40 subjects in each treatment group and 40 in each control group. If we calculate the sample size needed to yield a power level of .95 ($\beta = \alpha = .05$) for an effect size of $.20\sigma$ (which, recall from Chapter 1, is equivalent to an 18% improvement in the "success" rate for the treatment group), we find that the treatment and control group must each have a minimum of almost

700 subjects for a total of about 1400 in both groups (see Chapter 4). In other words, if we wish to increase power through sample size alone in this instance, sample size must increase approximately 1650% over the average for present practice in order to attain a power level that makes Type II error as small as the conventional limit on Type I error. Even attaining the much more modest .80 power level suggested by Cohen ($\beta = .20$) in this case would require a sample size of about 400 per experimental group, a tenfold increase over present practice.

Researchers are certainly aware of the importance of large samples in treatment effectiveness research. The fact that insufficient samples are nonetheless widely used in such research, therefore, must indicate how difficult it is to obtain the relatively large samples required. Thus while increased sample size is an effective means to increase statistical power and should be used whenever feasible, cost and availability of subjects may restrict the researcher's ability to use this approach. It is important, therefore, that the researcher be aware of alternative routes to increasing statistical power. Part II of this volume is devoted to identifying such alternative routes.

Effect Size

Other things being equal, the larger the effect produced by the treatment on a given dependent variable for the population, the more likely it is that statistical significance will be attained and the greater the statistical power. The role of effect size in the statistical power of treatment effectiveness research is especially problematic. One problem is the difficulty of knowing what effect size is reasonable to expect from a treatment under investigation so that research can be planned with sufficient power to detect it if present. Chapter 3 is devoted to consideration of this matter.

A second and related problem has to do with the "relativity" of effect size in treatment effectiveness research (Sechrest & Yeaton, 1982). For a given dependent measure and a given difference between the treatment condition and the control condition on that measure, the effect size will be larger or smaller depending on the relative values of the difference between the means, on the one hand, and the variance, on the other. Factors that affect either term in relation to the other can drastically alter the overall effect size. Figure 2.2 depicts this situation. In panel A the population variance is relatively large and the means of the two conditions differ by .5 standard deviations ($ES = .50$). In panel B the same difference between means for the same variable yields an ES of 1.2 because of the smaller common variance in the treatment and control distributions. In panel C the

A

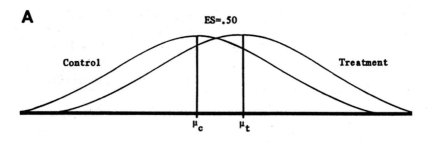

B

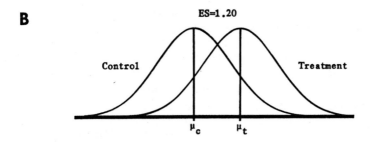

C

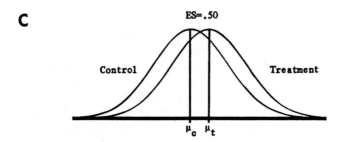

Figure 2.2: Graphical Depiction of the Manner in Which the Effect Size Is Dependent on the Relative Magnitude of the Difference between the Means and the Variance

distributions have the same variance as panel B, but the difference between the means is less, resulting again in an effect size of .50.

This relativity is one of the features that makes the effect size element of statistical power problematic in applied treatment effectiveness research. Suppose that for such research we hypothesize some "true" value of the effect size representing treatment and control conditions ideally implemented on full populations with results that are perfectly measured. We would hope that the effect size estimate a researcher ends up with in a study of that treatment would be a reasonably close approximation to this true value. Unfortunately, there are many ways to fall short of the ideal in treatment effectiveness research and nearly all of them work to lower effect size estimates in relation to such true values.

Two sets of such issues must be considered, corresponding respectively to the effect size numerator and denominator. First, if there is degradation of the treatment so that it achieves less than its full potential effect or if the expression of that effect is limited by the measure used, the numerator of the effect size ratio shrinks, making for a smaller total value. Second, if there are extraneous influences on dependent variable scores, the variability of those scores will generally be increased and the denominator of the effect size ratio will be inflated, again making for a smaller total value. Since degradation of treatment, insensitive measures, and extraneous sources of variance are not uncommon in treatment effectiveness research, effect size estimates made from such research can be severely diminished relative to "true" population values with devastating consequences for statistical power (see Boruch & Gomez, 1977). It is worthwhile to consider treatment issues and variability issues separately in somewhat more detail.

Treatment effectiveness research begins with a treatment concept which is believed to have potential for producing certain effects. Operationalization of that concept in a research design involves two important steps. First, a treatment plan must be formulated. A treatment plan specifies the particular activities, procedures, dosages, and so forth that the researcher intends to have administered to the respective experimental conditions. Of interest in this context is the "strength" of the treatment reflected in that plan (Yeaton & Sechrest, 1981). A given treatment concept can be tested with treatment plans that range from a weak or minimal representation of the concept to a very strong one. In psychotherapy, for example, the most experienced therapists can be used to provide an intense treatment over a long duration or student interns might be used to provide occasional treatment over a short term. In medicine, treatment strength is often represented by the dosage level of the drugs administered (amount and frequency). The problem for treatment effectiveness research is that, as a practical matter, weaker treatments are generally easier and cheaper to mount and, of course, are likely to have smaller effects. Thus the effect size in a treatment effectiveness study can be small because a weak version of the treatment concept was used which underrepresented its potential.

Second, given a treatment plan (strong or weak), the specified treatment must be delivered to each subject in the treatment condition and withheld from each subject in the control condition. In practical treatment effectiveness research such uniformity can be very difficult to achieve. At issue here is the "integrity" of the treatment, the extent to which the specified treatment plan was fully delivered or implemented (Boruch & Gomez, 1977; Yeaton & Sechrest, 1981). For example, the treatment plan might call for a sample of ex-convicts each to receive regular peer counseling of a specified sort. The convicts may be difficult to locate, however, and may not persist in counseling if located. As a result, relatively few of the targeted clients may receive any counseling at all, and those that do may receive considerably less than planned (see Rezmovic, Cook, & Dobson, 1981). Such degradations of treatment integrity, which are not at all uncommon in treatment effectiveness research, constitute a double disadvantage for statistical power. On the one hand, as weak treatments they reduce the absolute size of the difference between treated and untreated groups, lowering effect size via the numerator of the effect size ratio. On the other hand, such degradation is usually not uniform—some subjects receive more treatment than do others. This has the result of increasing the variability in dependent variable scores and further lowers the effect size via the denominator of the effect size ratio.

The measures chosen to assess response to treatment can also influence the effect size numerator. For example, measures with low ceilings or high floors for the subject samples chosen may limit the extent to which the means for different experimental conditions are able to differ. Similarly, measures with overly coarse units, analogous to pounds or even tons instead of ounces, may obscure real contrast between treatment and control conditions. Even more fundamental, measures that lack validity for measuring the characteristic that is expected to change under treatment will not, of course, show differences between experimental groups whatever the efficacy of the treatment.

The denominator of the effect size ratio (the error variance component), in turn, may vary with the nature and circumstances of dependent variable measurement, with the characteristics of the subject population selected, and with the design of the research itself as well as with the integrity of the treatment manipulations. Much more will be said about this matter in Part II of this volume. For now, an overview will be offered for each of the major issues.

Consider first the measurement issues. These fall into two categories— those having to do with the selection of a dependent measure and those having to do with its administration. Certain characteristics of the dependent variable will greatly influence how dispersed the scores are. For example, more unreliable measures, other things being equal, have more variability. Also, criterion referenced or mastery type measures generally have less dispersion than do psychometric or individual differences type measures (Carver, 1974). The administration of dependent measures, in turn, affects the variance of scores when it is not uniform for all subjects. Self-administered instruments that challenge the literacy of respondents, inconsistent instructions or recording practices, circumstances that differentially motivate subjects' responses, and a host of other such factors will increase the spread of scores and reduce the effect size estimate.

Another important factor in the variability of scores on the dependent measure is the heterogeneity of the subject population at issue. Where dependent variables are related to stable subject characteristics, for example, gender, age, socio-economic status, personality, and so forth or baseline values on those same variables, more heterogeneity on those characteristics will result in more dispersion on the dependent variable scores. At this point issues having to do with the effect size element in statistical power come into close relationship with those having to do with the role of the statistical test. As noted earlier, one important aspect of the statistical test is the specification of the relevant population and the nature of the sampling from that population as a basis for estimating sampling error. When there is a great deal of heterogeneity in the population associated with measurable characteristics, statistical models using blocking, covariates, and so forth alter the effect size formulation in ways that reduce the variance term in its denominator. What remains an issue, of course, is subject heterogeneity on the dependent measure that cannot easily be removed via its correlation with an identifiable and measurable covariate, for example, variation in the mood and motivation of subjects at the time of measurement that affects the scores.

Treatment effectiveness research, therefore, is susceptible to a number of degradations of treatment strength, treatment integrity, sampling, measurement, and experimental control that serve to diminish the effect size estimate that will result and, consequently, lower statistical power. As should be apparent, the effect size parameter in statistical power is both complex and important. Indeed, learning to deal with it is the key to designing treatment effectiveness research that is sensitive to treatment effects. Finding ways to enhance the operative effect size in such research ranks alongside (and perhaps ahead of) increased sample size as a means to improve statistical power. The next chapter further discusses the nature of this "problematic parameter" and Part II of this volume is in large part devoted to explaining various techniques and approaches that give the researcher greater control over its relativity.

3. Effect Size: The Problematic Parameter

Of the four factors that determine statistical power, effect size is the most problematic. For one thing, it is a more complicated concept than alpha, sample size, or the statistical test, and its meaning in a given research context is less clear. Moreover, while effect size is a somewhat idealized population parameter, in practice it must be estimated from sample data. As a result, those estimates can be quite susceptible to the influence of very specific features of the treatment implementation, measures, samples, and research design chosen for a particular study. The problem that is perhaps most responsible for inhibiting statistical power analysis in the design of treatment effectiveness research, however, is the fact that the effect size is generally both unknown and difficult to guess. A researcher can easily establish the statistical test, alpha level, and sample size for a research design or, at least, make an informed judgment about what is appropriate or available. But what effect size should the research be designed to detect? Answering that question requires an analysis which integrates information about the strength and integrity of the treatment to be implemented, the responsiveness of the dependent measures to that treatment, the amount and nature of variability in the dependent measures, and the magnitude of difference between experimental groups that is meaningful in the treatment context of interest.

While a full, a priori analysis of all these factors is usually not possible, there are various frameworks that can be constructed to support reasonable judgment about the minimal effect size a treatment effectiveness study should be designed to detect. That judgment, in turn, will permit statistical power to be considered in a systematic, and not just intuitive, manner during the design of treatment effectiveness research. Conversely, given a framework for judgment about effect size, the statistical results of treatment research can also be more readily interpreted after it is completed. Three frameworks for judging effect size will be reviewed here: the actuarial approach, the statistical translation approach, and the criterion group contrast approach.

The Actuarial Approach

If enough research exists similar to that of interest, a researcher can use the results of those other studies to create an actuarial base for effect sizes. Each study deemed relevant and of sufficient methodological quality to be trustworthy can be examined to determine the effect size estimate that resulted for various dependent measures, irrespective of statistical significance. The distribution of such effect size estimates can then be used as a basis for judging the likelihood that the research being planned will produce effects of specified size. That information, in turn, allows a researcher to design a study with adequate power to detect effects in the range in which they are actually likely to occur for the treatment. For example, a study could reliably detect 80% of the likely effects if it were designed to have sufficient power for the effect size at the 20th percentile of the effect size distribution.

Other than having sufficient research literature to draw upon, the major difficulty with the actuarial approach is extracting effect size estimates from studies that typically do not report their results in effect size terms. This, however, is exactly the problem faced in meta-analysis when a researcher attempts to obtain effect size estimates from each of a defined set of studies and do higher order analysis on them. Books and articles on meta-analysis technique, such as Glass, McGaw, and Smith (1981), Rosenthal (1984), and Holmes (1984), contain detailed information about how to estimate effect size from reported t-test values, levels of statistical significance, means and standard deviations, and so forth. For many applications, the equations found in Chapter 4 of the present volume may also be used.

The best illustrations of the actuarial approach to judging effect size, in fact, come from treatment areas where meta-analyses have already been conducted (Cordray & Sonnefeld, 1985). For example, Cordray and Orwin (1983) examined the range and distribution of effect size estimates that resulted from the Smith, Glass, and Miller (1980) meta-analysis of psychotherapy research (which incorporated the Smith & Glass, 1977, study mentioned in Chapter 1). That meta-analysis yielded over 1700 effect size estimates from nearly 500 comparison group studies (many using multiple dependent measures and hence producing multiple effect sizes). Table 3.1 displays the distribution of those effect size estimates as tallied by Cordray and Orwin.

From Table 3.1 we can see that, for psychotherapy research, the median effect size (50th percentile) over all studies and all dependent measures was

TABLE 3.1 Distribution of 1766 Effect Sizes Found in the Smith, Glass, and Miller Meta-Analysis of Psychotherapy Treatment Effectiveness Studies

Effect size (ES)	Cumulative proportion	Effect size (ES)	Cumulative proportion
−.50	.02	1.10	.75
−.40	.03	1.20	.78
−.30	.04	1.30	.81
−.20	.06	1.40	.83
−.10	.08	1.50	.86
0	.11	1.60	.88
.10	.16	1.70	.89
.20	.20	1.80	.90
.30	.25	1.90	.91
.40	.32	2.00	.92
.50	.39	2.10	.93
.60	.46	2.20	.93
.70	.54	2.30	.94
.80	.60	2.40	.96
.90	.66	2.50	.96
1.00	.71		

SOURCE: Adapted from Cordray and Orwin, 1983

around .65 standard deviations difference between treatment and control group. The 25th percentile of the effect size distribution was at a level of .30 standard deviation units and the 75th percentile was at $ES = 1.10$. Put the other way around, 75% of the studies yielded an effect size greater than .30 and 25% yielded one greater than 1.10. With this information in hand, a researcher planning a psychotherapy effectiveness study can make a reasonably good estimate of the likelihood of obtaining effects of different orders of magnitude. To ensure that any effect larger than, say, the 25th percentile value is detected, the research must be designed so that it has adequate statistical power for an effect as small as $ES = .30$.

Dozens of meta-analyses of psychological, educational, behavioral, and medical treatment effectiveness research have been conducted since the technique was introduced in the mid 1970s. A researcher has a reasonable chance of finding at least one meta-analysis covering a domain similar to a planned study with regard to type of treatment and dependent measures. Typically, meta-analyses report the overall mean of the effect sizes extracted from the studies at issue and the standard deviation (sometimes standard error) of those effect sizes. For a researcher planning treatment

TABLE 3.2 Percentiles of a Normal Distribution in Relation to the
              Standard Deviation

Percentile	Deviation from $\bar{X}$ in sd units	Percentile	Deviation from $\bar{X}$ in sd units
0	< − 2.50	50	0
5	− 1.64	55	+ .13
10	− 1.28	60	+ .25
15	− 1.04	65	+ .39
20	− .84	70	+ .52
25	− .67	75	+ .67
30	− .52	80	+ .84
35	− .39	85	+ 1.04
40	− .25	90	+ 1.28
45	− .13	95	+ 1.64
		100	> + 2.50

effectiveness research, it is more useful to have the effect size distribution
displayed in cumulative proportion or percentile terms, as for the psychotherapy results presented in Table 3.1. If we assume a normal distribution,
it is relatively easy to convert information about the mean and standard
deviation of the effect size distribution into percentiles, as shown in Table
3.2. If, for instance, we knew that the mean effect size from a meta-
analysis was .50 and the standard deviation of the distribution of effect
sizes (s) was 0.6, consulting Table 3.2 would tell us that the 25th percentile
of that distribution was .67s below its mean, that is, $\bar{X} - .67(s)$ or, in this
case .50 − .67(0.6) = .10. Hence, for this example, 75% of the effect size
estimates obtained by the studies incorporated in the meta-analysis were
.10 or larger.

If a meta-analysis reports the standard error (se) of the effect size distribution instead of the standard deviation, it can be converted to standard
deviation form as follows: $s = se\sqrt{m-1}$ where m is the number of effect
sizes in the distribution. With this adjustment, Table 3.2 can be used as in
the example above.

We can paint a still more general picture of the range and magnitude of
effect size estimates in treatment effectiveness research by examining the
results of a number of meta-analyses simultaneously. As mentioned in
Chapter 1, the author has collected reports of 186 meta-analyses that have
been conducted on psychological, educational, and behavioral treatment
effectiveness research. Table 3.3 lists the treatment areas represented in this
set of meta-analyses. Beside each entry in that table are one or more index
numbers which identify the corresponding bibliographic entry in the refer-

TABLE 3.3 Treatment Areas and Reference Numbers for 186
Meta-Analyses of Treatment Effectiveness Research

Mental Health

　Psychotherapy

Psychotherapy, general (6, 24, 28, 108, 127, 145, 146, 162, 163, 171, 176, 191)
Cognitive behavior therapy; behavior modification (15, 45, 124, 141, 151)

　Counseling, Psycho-Educational Treatment, Specialized Therapy

Community-based mental health alternatives, innovative outpatient programs (178)
Prevention programs in mental health (11, 175, 179)
Treatment by paraprofessionals in mental health, education, law, and social work (183)
Training in interpersonal cognitive problem-solving skills (4, 40)
Family therapy; marriage enrichment; parent effectiveness training (27, 58, 68, 188)
Meditation and relaxation techniques (16, 48, 52)
Assertiveness training (18, 164)
Therapeutic interventions with juvenile delinquents (55, 56, 61, 83)
Adolescent drug prevention programs (182)
Therapy for test anxiety (44, 131)
Guidance and counseling programs in high school (10, 173)
Mental practice of motor skills (51)

　Health Related Psychological or Educational Treatment

Education/counseling for medical patients (42, 43, 67, 77, 121, 126, 142, 143)
Psychosocial preventive care for the elderly (194)
Adolescent pregnancy education programs (78)
Childbirth, new infant instruction for adults (81, 184)
Biofeedback and relaxation training for headaches (16)
Tobacco smoking cessation/reduction programs (50)
Behavioral treatment for obesity (132)
Nutrition education programs (109)
Feingold diet (free of food additives) for children (88)
Treatment for stuttering (5)

　Work Setting or Organizational Interventions

Psychologically-based organizational intervention (64)
Job enrichment or work redesign (122)
Realistic job previews before entering organization (122, 149)
Personnel training programs (20, 49)

Education

　General Education, K-12 and College

　　Instructional programs or techniques

Computer-assisted instruction (14, 21, 93, 101, 104, 128, 160)
Programmed or individualized instruction (2, 3, 12, 66, 74, 95, 102, 106, 158)

(continued)

TABLE 3.3 (*continued*)

Audio-tutorial or visual-based instruction (30, 103, 157)
Simulation games in instruction (39, 181)
Behavioral objectives, reinforcement, cues, feedback, etc. (8, 114, 115, 116)
Teacher use of higher vs. lower level questions (148)
Group-based, teacher-paced mastery learning strategies (63)
Cooperative task structures (23, 79, 80)
School-based tutoring (31, 37, 140)
Home instruction supported by school-based programs (62)
Assignment of homework (137)

Study and recall aids/techniques

Hierarchical sequence of material for learning (76)
Aids for helping students select important aspects of material (75, 90, 113)
Advance organizers for instructional material (91, 92, 110, 111, 112, 177)
Illustrated instructional material; graphic organizers (7, 125, 147)
Manipulative materials, hand calculators in teaching mathematics (70, 136)
Instruction to use imagery to aid recall (144)
Lecture notetaking and reviewing notes (71)

Classroom organization

Open classroom vs. traditional plan (57, 72, 117, 138)
Small class size vs. large class size (59, 69, 170)
Between- and within-class ability grouping (96, 97, 98, 129, 169)

Feedback to teachers

Feedback to teachers about academic performance of students (54)
Feedback of student ratings to teachers (29)

Coaching on test taking

Coaching programs for test performance (13, 41, 94, 100, 123, 154, 161)
Test anxiety; familiar vs. unfamiliar examiner (44, 53, 131)

Specific Instructional or Content Areas

Science and math instructional programs

Instructional systems/curricula in science/math (9, 19, 107, 165, 166, 167, 190, 192)
Individualized instruction in science courses (2, 3, 66, 74)
Computer-assisted mathematics instruction (21)
Science/math teaching techniques (17, 33, 38, 46, 47, 70, 75, 110, 119, 136, 180, 195, 196, 197)

Special content other than science and math

Reading improvement or study skills programs (139, 156, 174)
Instructional programs for teaching writing (73)
Accelerated instruction for gifted students (99)
Creativity training (32, 152)
Moral training; primary prevention programs in schools (11, 159)

TABLE 3.3 (*continued*)

Career education programs; guidance counseling (10, 11, 173)
Nutrition education programs (109)

Preschool and Special Education; Developmental Disabilities

Early intervention for disadvantaged or handicapped (1, 25, 26, 34, 60, 185)
Special education programs or classrooms (22, 172, 189)
Tutoring of special education students (37, 140)
Computer-assisted instruction for special education students (160)
Cooperative learning, handicapped or ethnically different students (23, 79)
Training for mentally retarded persons on memory and learning tasks (120)
Perceptual-motor treatment for developmental disabilities (87, 89, 133, 134, 135)
Educational programs for behaviorally disordered students (153, 168)
Remedial language programs; bilingual instruction (84, 85, 86, 130, 193)
Programs for high risk and disadvantaged college students (105)

Teacher Training

Inservice training for teachers (47, 65, 82, 150, 180, 186, 187, 197)
Practice or field experience during teacher training (35, 36, 118, 155)

NOTE: Citations for the meta-analyses upon which this table is based are listed, by number, in the reference appendix to this volume.

ence appendix to this volume. These citations are intended to aid a reader who wishes to locate meta-analyses that may be of relevance to designing research in a particular treatment area.

Constructing the cumulative distribution of mean effect size estimates from these meta-analyses provides a display of the range within which the results of any such treatment effectiveness research will likely fall. Table 3.4 presents such a distribution for 102 of the mean effect sizes reported in the meta-analyses listed in Table 3.3. These 102 mean effect sizes were selected by the following criteria:

1. When two or more meta-analyses covered largely overlapping sets of studies, only one mean effect size was taken, specifically, that representing the meta-analysis with the broadest coverage (largest number of studies).
2. When mean effect sizes were reported for different categories of dependent measures, only that for the primary category was taken, for example, learning outcomes for educational interventions rather than attitude change.
3. Mean effect sizes were taken only if they were based largely or exclusively on comparison group studies, that is, treatment versus control; in particular, mean effect sizes based on pretreatment-posttreatment comparisons with no control group were eliminated (these effect sizes are characteristically larger than those based on comparison groups).
4. Mean effect sizes were taken only if they were based on both published and unpublished studies (published studies characteristically have larger effect

TABLE 3.4 Cumulative Distribution of 102 Selected Mean Effect
Sizes Drawn from 186 Meta-Analyses of Treatment
Effectiveness Research

Mean effect size ($\overline{ES}$)	Cumulative proportion			
−.10	.01			
−.05	.02			
.00	.02			
.05	.02			
.10	.07			
.15	.13			
.20	.19			
.25	.25			
.30	.32			
.35	.45			
.40	.50			
.45	.55	Summary statistics:		
.50	.60			
.55	.68	Grand mean	.45	
.60	.73	N	102	
.65	.76	SD	.26	
.70	.83			
.75	.89			
.80	.91			
.85	.92			
.90	.94			
.95	.95			
1.00	.97			
1.05	.98			
1.10	.99			
1.15	.99			
1.20	1.00			

sizes than unpublished ones, likely due to bias in the publication process
favoring statistically significant results).

5. Two outliers on the positive side of the distribution were excluded.

Additionally, it should be noted that the majority of the treatment meta-
analyses listed in Table 3.3 have been conducted in education. The distribution of those mean effect sizes meeting the above criteria was quite similar for the education and noneducation meta-analyses, however, so they
are combined in Table 3.4. The 102 mean effect sizes in this combined
distribution summarize the results of about 6700 individual treatment effectiveness studies involving nearly 800,000 subjects.

The most striking aspect of Table 3.4 is the strong positive skew to the distribution of mean effect sizes. With remarkably few exceptions, these 102 effect size estimates show positive treatment effects (though sometimes only slightly positive). That is, most of these meta-analyses found that, in the aggregate, treated groups did better on the dependent variables employed than did the control groups with which they were compared. The grand mean for the overall distribution is .45, meaning that, on average, the treatment group scores on the dependent variable were nearly half a standard deviation better than those of the comparison group. It is important to keep in mind that meta-analysis only summarizes whatever statistical effects appeared in the studies included in the meta-analysis. Those effects, in turn, may be biased by any methodological inadequacies of those original studies. Thus while selected meta-analysis results provide some idea of what has been found in a treatment area, given conventional research practices in that area, they may be a misleading indication of what would be found if all studies met higher methodological standards.

We can, nonetheless, use the results depicted in Table 3.4 to draw some general rules of thumb about the effects we might be trying to detect in the general case of treatment effectiveness research in the behavioral sciences. Recall that Cohen (1977, 1988) suggested that, across a wide range of such research, reasonable guidelines were to judge $ES = .20$ as a "small" effect, .50 as "medium," and .80 as "large." With the meta-analysis results in Table 3.4 we can give a more empirically detailed set of guidelines for the specific domain of treatment effectiveness research in the behavioral sciences. To do this, we will more or less arbitrarily call the lower 33% of the *positive* effect sizes found in the meta-analyses "small," the middle 34% "medium," and the largest 33% "large." Thus we are saying that, relative to the range of effects actually reported for such research, the middle third of the distribution is what we mean by medium while more extreme values will be judged, respectively, as small or large. Using these definitions, Table 3.5 reports the small, medium, and large segments of the distribution of mean effect size estimates in Table 3.4.

The midpoint of each of the effect size ranges in Table 3.5 may be the best summary value to use as a rule of thumb in treatment effectiveness research. A researcher who designs a study to have a given power for one of those midpoint effect size values will have greater power for effect size values larger than the midpoint and less power for values smaller than the midpoint. Over the selected range, however, the average power should be approximately that determined for the midpoint value (excluding effect sizes close to zero).

Table 3.5, therefore, tells us that a researcher who wishes to be able to

TABLE 3.5 "Small," "Medium," and "Large" Positive Effect Size Ranges
Based on 102 Selected Mean Effect Sizes from 186
Meta-Analyses of Treatment Effectiveness Research

Range	Values of ES	Midpoint[a]
"Small" (lower 33%)	.00 to .32	.15
"Medium" (middle 34%)	.33 to .55	.45
"Large" (upper 33%)	.56 to 1.20	.90

[a]Rounded to the nearest .05.

detect a small treatment effect should design the research study to have
adequate power for $ES = .15$. Similarly, a researcher wishing to detect a
medium effect would design the study for $ES = .45$ and, for a large effect,
design for $ES = .90$. These values are fairly close to Cohen's guidelines
(.20, .50, and .80, respectively) and therefore offer little improvement on
his advice. It is worth noting, however, that small effects in treatment effectiveness research are often smaller than Cohen indicated from his broader
sampling of social science research. Because of the particular difficulty of
detecting small effects, the researcher working in this range might take
extra care to ensure adequate power.

The Statistical Translation Approach

As shown in Chapter 2, expressing effect size in standard deviation units
has the advantage of staying close to the terms in statistical significance
testing and thus facilitates statistical power analysis. That formulation,
however, has the disadvantage that in many treatment domains we have
little basis for intuition about the practical meaning of a standard deviation's worth of difference between experimental groups. One approach to
this difficulty is to translate the effect size index (ES) from standard deviation units to some alternate form that is easier to assess. That alternate form
may make it easier to anticipate the size of an effect, as an aid to designing
power into a study, or to judge the size of an effect after it is obtained.

Perhaps the easiest translation is simply to express the effect size in the
units of the dependent measure of interest, that is, to use the "unstandardized" effect size. The ES index, recall, is the difference between the means
of the experimental groups divided by the pooled standard deviations of
the groups. Previous research, norms for standardized tests, or pilot research is often capable of providing a reasonable value for the relevant

standard deviation. With that value in hand, any level of *ES* a researcher is considering can be converted to the metric of the specific variable by multiplying by the standard deviation and, conversely, any meaningful unstandardized difference between means can be converted to the *ES* index by dividing by the standard deviation. For example, if the dependent variable of interest is a standardized reading achievement test, for which the norms indicate a standard deviation of 15 points on samples similar to those of interest, the researcher can think of *ES* = .50 as 7.5 points on that test and vice versa. In context it may be easier to judge the practical magnitude of 7.5 points on a well-known measure than it is to judge .50 standard deviations.

In addition, the *ES* index can be readily converted to proportion of variance terms (*PV*) and, from there, to an independent variable/dependent variable correlation:

$$PV = r^2 = \frac{ES^2}{ES^2 + 4} \qquad r = \frac{ES}{\sqrt{ES^2 + 4}}$$

Conversely:

$$ES = \frac{2r}{\sqrt{1 - r^2}} = \sqrt{\frac{4(PV)}{1 - (PV)}}$$

The proportion of variance form of the effect size and, most particularly, the correlation between the independent variable and the dependent variable are common indices of strength of association. Many researchers, therefore, may be comfortable thinking about them. Table 3.6 translates a range of *ES* values into various alternate formulations (including some to be discussed later). Columns (1) and (2) of that table represent translation to proportions of variance (*PV*) and correlation coefficients (*r*).

The proportion of variance formulation, however, does not necessarily represent much improvement over the *ES* index in many research domains. Indeed, *PV* can be downright misleading. With an index in proportion or percentage terms, one naturally expects something around 1.00 or 100% to be the large end of the effect-size scale (or, analogously, a correlation of 1.00). Since much of the variance on dependent measures in treatment research often has sources unaffected by treatment, the maximum possible treatment effect in *PV* terms can be considerably less than 100%. Under

TABLE 3.6 Effect Size Equivalents for *ES*, *PV*, *r*, *U3*, and BESD

ES	(1) PV (r^2)	(2) r	(3) U3: % of T above $\bar{X}_c$	(4) BESD C vs. T success rates		(5) BESD C vs. T differential
0.1	.002	.05	54	.47	.52	.05
0.2	.01	.10	58	.45	.55	.10
0.3	.02	.15	62	.42	.57	.15
0.4	.04	.20	66	.40	.60	.20
0.5	.06	.24	69	.38	.62	.24
0.6	.08	.29	73	.35	.64	.29
0.7	.11	.33	76	.33	.66	.33
0.8	.14	.37	79	.31	.68	.37
0.9	.17	.41	82	.29	.70	.41
1.0	.20	.45	84	.27	.72	.45
1.1	.23	.48	86	.26	.74	.48
1.2	.26	.51	88	.24	.75	.51
1.3	.30	.54	90	.23	.77	.54
1.4	.33	.57	92	.21	.78	.57
1.5	.36	.60	93	.20	.80	.60
1.6	.39	.62	95	.19	.81	.62
1.7	.42	.65	96	.17	.82	.65
1.8	.45	.67	96	.16	.83	.67
1.9	.47	.69	97	.15	.84	.69
2.0	.50	.71	98	.14	.85	.71
2.1	.52	.72	98	.14	.86	.72
2.2	.55	.74	99	.13	.87	.74
2.3	.57	.75	99	.12	.87	.75
2.4	.59	.77	99	.11	.88	.77
2.5	.61	.78	99	.11	.89	.78
2.6	.63	.79	99	.10	.89	.79
2.7	.65	.80	99	.10	.90	.80
2.8	.66	.81	99	.09	.90	.81
2.9	.68	.82	99	.09	.91	.82
3.0	.69	.83	99	.08	.91	.83

such circumstances, numerically small *PV* values can represent effects that are really of considerable practical significance.

Often what we want to know about the magnitude of an effect is not the strength of the statistical relation represented, but what it means in terms of the proportion of people who attained a given level of benefit as a result of treatment. One attractive way to depict effect size, therefore, is in terms of the proportion of the treatment group, in comparison to the control group, elevated over some success threshold by the treatment. This requires, of course, that we be able to set some reasonable criterion for success on the dependent variable scale, but even a relatively arbitrary threshold value can be used to illustrate the nature of the difference between treatment and control groups.

If we already have treatment versus control group data on the dependent variable of interest, the procedure is straightforward. We merely determine the proportion of the control group and the proportion of the treatment group above the success threshold set on that dependent variable. For example, suppose a self-esteem scale has been normed so that we know the mean for "normal" high school students is 50 points. We might then set 50 as a reasonable standard of success for a group of dropouts whose self-esteem we are trying to improve through assertion training. We divide the posttreatment scores of the treatment group into those above and those below 50 and do likewise for the control group. The results can be depicted in a chart such as Table 3.7. The fictitious data presented there show that after treatment the mean difference between the treatment group and the control group amounted to an increase from 32% to 44% in the proportion of students considered a success on the self-esteem variable. Alternatively, note that the failure rate has been reduced from 68% to 56% by the treatment. These versions of the effect size may be more meaningful in context than merely to note that the difference represents $ES = .25$ in standard deviation units which, in fact, it does.

The example above requires that we already have experimental data. For the researcher who wants to think about expected effect size in success rate terms in advance of the experiment—for example, so that adequate statistical power can be designed into the study—a different approach must be used. First, a success rate table such as Table 3.7 must be constructed for the hypothetical case of the smallest success rate differential between treatment and control group the researcher wants to be able to detect. Then that success rate configuration must be converted to the ES index so that it can be used in statistical power computations. For example, with a stipulated success threshold a researcher may know that an untreated control can be expected to have a success rate of, say, 30%. The researcher may further believe that an improvement to, say, 40% is about the smallest gain worth detecting in the context of the particular research.

To compute the ES index in standard deviation units, the success rate information must first be converted to another statistic, then that statistic converted to ES. Both the 2×2 Chi-square and the fourfold point correlation coefficient (appropriate for relations between two dichotomous variables) can be used for that purpose. Computational procedures for these statistics are widely available in introductory statistics books (see Hays, 1973). The conversion from those statistics to ES can be made using the following formulas:

TABLE 3.7 Example of a Dichotomous Success Rate Chart Constructed
for Posttreatment Data on a Given Dependent Variable

	Control group		Treatment group	
	n	(%)	n	(%)
Success (>50 pts)	8	(32)	11	(44)
Failure (<50 pts)	17	(68)	14	(56)

NOTE: Fictitious data

$$ES = \frac{2r_{fp}}{\sqrt{1 - (r_{fp})^2}} \qquad ES = \sqrt{\frac{4(X^2)}{N - (X^2)}}$$

Where r_{fp} is the fourfold point correlation coefficient computed between the success dichotomy and the group dichotomy, X^2 is the Chi-square value for the 2×2 success rate table, and N is the total number of subjects (both groups combined) in that Chi-square table.

A simpler practical technique for converting success rate tables to the ES index, however, is to transform the treatment group success proportion and the control group success proportion to arcsine values and difference them (Cohen, 1977, chap. 6). That difference can be read directly as ES. (Table 4.1 in Chapter 4 of this volume provides the needed arcsine values.)

A more general approach to expressing effect size in success rate terms is to set the mean of the control group distribution as the success threshold value of interest. With symmetrical normal distributions, 50% of the control distribution will be below that point and 50% will be above. These proportions can be compared with those of the treatment group distribution below and above the same point for any given difference between the two distributions in standard deviation units. Figure 3.1 depicts the relationship for an effect size of $ES = .50$. In this case, 70% of the treatment group is above the mean of the control group or, in failure rate terms, only 30% of the treated group is below the control group mean. An alternate statement of this same relation, incidentally, is to say that the treatment group mean is at the 70th percentile of the control group distribution. In other words, the average subject in the treated group has a score higher than 70% of the untreated subjects.

There are various ways to construct indices of the overlap between distributions to represent effect size (Cohen, 1977, p. 21). The one described

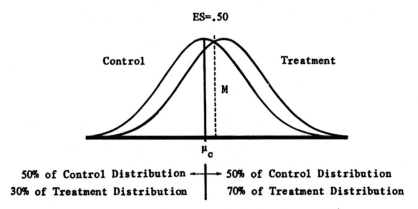

Figure 3.1: Depiction of the Percent of the Treatment Distribution above the Success Threshold Set at the Mean of the Control Distribution

above corresponds to Cohen's *U3* measure. *U3* is defined as the percentage of the control distribution exceeded by the upper 50% of the treatment population. Thus for the above case, *U3* = 70% since the mean of the treatment distribution (50% point) falls at the 70th percentile of the control distribution. With normal, symmetrical, equal-sized populations, *U3* is both the percent of the control distribution below the treatment mean and the percent of the treatment distribution above the control mean. Table 3.6 (presented earlier) provides the equivalencies between the effect size in standard deviation units and the *U3* percent nonoverlap index in column (3).

A variation on the percent nonoverlap index has been offered by Rosenthal and Rubin (1982) who used it to construct something they called a "binomial effect size display" (BESD). They suggested that, for purposes of illustrating effect size, the success threshold be presumed to be at the grand median for the conjoint control and treatment distribution (Line M in Figure 3.1). Though using the grand median as a success threshold is somewhat arbitrary, note that when there is no effect, the grand median coincides with the individual medians of each distribution. Thus this standard presumes a 50–50 success-failure split when there is no effect and a widening difference when there is.

The advantage of the BESD approach is that with normal distributions the difference between the "success" proportions of the treatment and control groups has a simple relationship to the effect size expressed in correlational or proportion of variance terms. In particular, when we express effect size as a correlation (r), the value of that correlation corresponds to the difference between the proportions of the respective distributions that are above the grand median success threshold. Thus if the correlation between the independent variable and the dependent variable is .24 ($ES = .50$), then the difference between the success proportions of the groups is .24 evenly divided around the .50 point, that is, .50 plus or minus .12, or 38% success in the control group, 62% in the treatment group. More generally, the distribution with the lower mean will have $.50 - (r/2)$ of its cases above the grand median success threshold and the distribution with the greater mean will have $.50 + (r/2)$ of its cases above that threshold.

Since ES can be readily converted to r, the BESD proportions are very easy to determine. Unlike the $U3$ measure described earlier, they do not require the researcher to work directly with the areas under the normal curve, nor do they require that a table be consulted in order to transform a particular ES or r effect size into success rate terms. For convenience, however, Table 3.6 (presented earlier) shows in columns (4) and (5) the conversion to BESD terms for a range of ES and r values.

The most striking thing about the BESD and, for that matter, the $U3$ representation of the effect size is the different impression they give of the potential practical significance of a given effect from that of the standard deviation or percent of variance expression. For example, an effect size of one-fifth of a standard deviation ($ES = .20$) corresponds to an r^2 of .01. That is, the treatment "accounts for" only one percent of the variance on the dependent variable. This statement implies that the treatment effect is really quite small, almost trivial—after all, 99% of the variance remains unaccounted for.

The BESD success rate differential for that same effect, however, is .10, that is, 10 percentage points separate the treatment from the control group. Using the grand median as the presumed success criterion, 45% of the control group and 55% of the treatment group are successful. A 10-percentage-point success increase on a control group baseline of 45% success represents a 22% improvement in the success rate (10/45). Viewed in these terms, the same treatment effect that appeared trivial as a proportion of total variance now looks potentially quite meaningful. In a world where 10% is judged a good return on an investment, a treatment that produces more than a 20% increase in the success rate sounds almost impressive.

Whatever the particular index favored, the merit of the translation approach is that it allows effect size to be converted to a form that may be easier to interpret in a particular research context. A statistical finding in ES terms can be converted, for example, to a success rate differential to get a better "feel" for what it means. Conversely, a researcher may find it easier to judge what effect size his or her research should be designed to detect if it is first framed in some more interpretable form, then translated into *ES* for purposes of considering and computing statistical power.

The Criterion Group Contrast Approach

While actuarial and statistical translation approaches to assessing effect size may be useful for many purposes, they are generally somewhat removed from the specific context of any given treatment effectiveness study. Often, the best answer to the question of what effect size has practical significance is one that is closely tied to the particular problems, populations, and measures relevant to the treatment under investigation. For example, if we could identify and measure a naturally occurring effect in the problem context whose practical significance was easily recognized, it could be used as a criterion value or benchmark against which any expected or obtained treatment effect could be compared.

An "effect," for our purposes, is a between-groups difference on a dependent measure of interest for treatment research. What is required in the criterion group contrast approach is that some such comparison be identified, preferably one with intuitive meaning and familiar practical value, and represented as a statistical effect size on the dependent measure relevant to treatment effectiveness research. Since this effect size should correspond to a difference of known practical significance, it can then serve as a standard against which to compare or anticipate any other less well-anchored effect.

The criterion group contrast approach is best explained by example. Consider a community mental health center in which prospective patients receive a routine diagnostic intake interview and are sorted into those judged to need, say, inpatient therapy versus outpatient therapy. This practice embodies a discrimination of more serious from less serious cases and the "size" of the difference between the severity of the symptoms for these two groups would be well understood at the practical level by those involved in community mental health settings. If we administered a functional status measure that was of interest as an outcome variable for treatment research to both these groups, we could represent the difference between them as an effect size, that is, the difference between their means on that measure divided by the pooled standard deviations. Though this "effect size" does not represent the effects of treatment, we can nonetheless think of it in comparison with a treatment effect. That is, how successful would we judge a treatment that, when applied to clients as severe as the inpatient group, left them with scores similar to those of the outpatient group? Such an effect would most likely be judged to be of considerable practical significance and would have recognized meaning in the treatment context. Real or anticipated treatment effects can thus be compared with this criterion contrast value as a way of judging their practical significance.

Another example comes from Carver's (1975) analysis of the effects of school characteristics on students' reading achievement. By comparing the reading achievement test scores of fifth grade pupils with those of sixth grade pupils, Carver invoked a criterion group contrast that represented a difference or gain of recognizable magnitude in the elementary school setting. That difference, in turn, translated into an effect size equivalent to 1.8% of the total variance in reading achievement test scores. Thus, though modest sounding, 1.8% of the variance in this case was judged worthwhile ($ES = .27$). By comparison with this benchmark, Carver further judged that the 10% of the variance in reading scores that was related to variation in school characteristics in the Coleman Report (Coleman et al., 1966) also represented a relationship of practical significance despite its modest numerical magnitude.

Reasonable criterion comparisons are often surprisingly easy to find in applied treatment settings. Indeed, in many cases descriptive data using variables relevant to assessing treatment outcome are routinely obtained from participants—for example, achievement test scores for school children, symptom checklists for mental health patients, and so forth. All that is needed to create a criterion contrast are, first, two groups whose difference on the variable of interest is easily recognized and, second, the results of measurement on that variable. It is also desirable to use groups which resemble, as much as possible, those samples likely to be used in any actual treatment research. In particular, the variability within the groups should be comparable to that likely for research samples, and the order of magnitude of their between-groups difference should be within the range for which treatment effects might reasonably be expected. Some of the possibilities for criterion contrasts that frequently occur in practical settings include:

1. Eligible versus ineligible applicants for service where eligibility is primarily determined on the basis of judged need or severity. For example, a contrast on economic status might compare those who did not quality for food stamps with those who did.

2. Sorting of treatment recipients into different service or diagnostic categories based on the severity of the problems to be treated. For example, a contrast

on literacy might compare those adult education students enrolled in remedial reading classes versus those enrolled in other kinds of classes.

3. Categories of termination status after treatment. For example, a contrast on functional status measures might compare those patients judged by physical therapists to have had highly successful outcomes versus those judged to have had very unsuccessful outcomes.

4. Comparison of "normal" subjects with those who have the target problem. For example, a contrast on delinquent behavior could compare the frequency of self-reported delinquency for a sample of males arrested by the police with similarly-aged males from an unselected high school sample.

5. Maturational differences and/or those occurring with "normal" or usual treatments. For example, a contrast on mathematics achievement might compare the achievement test scores of third graders with those of fifth graders.

The following example more specifically illustrates the use of criterion group contrasts:

In the study of juvenile delinquency treatment, the most common and important outcome measure is recidivism, that is, whether a juvenile has further contact with the police or juvenile courts after treatment (or the number of such contacts). It is of interest to know how much of a change (or difference) in recidivism has practical meaning in the context of the juvenile justice system.

To provide some basis for judgment during the course of a series of quasi-experiments on the treatment of minor offenders, the author constructed a contrast on various recidivism measures using two groups of delinquents whose differences were already familiar within the juvenile justice system (Lipsey, Cordray, & Berger, 1981; Lipsey, 1983). When a juvenile is arrested, there are generally three possible dispositions the police can make, depending upon the seriousness of the offense and the prior delinquent history. They can have the juvenile kept in custody pending juvenile court action, they can refer the case to the probation department for official processing but not custody, or they can "counsel and release" the juvenile to the parents. These three dispositions embody a kind of "seriousness of delinquency" scale for which the different categories have real practical meaning to law enforcement officials.

Since the delinquency treatment research at issue focused on the lower end of the seriousness continuum, that is, minor and moderate offenders, a criterion contrast was constructed between noncustody probation referrals and juveniles counseled and released. The difference in recidivism between these two groups of juveniles was presumed to be a meaningful benchmark for judging practical treatment effects. A treatment effect equivalent to reducing recidivism rates from the level of the probation noncustody group to the level of the counsel and release group would be moderately large and of recognizable value in this context.

The difference between these two criterion groups on a recidivism measure counting the frequency of arrests over the six-month period subsequent to the initial police disposition corresponded to an ES of .26. With Table 3.6 and some interpolation we can translate this value as $r = .13$ or, in BESD terms, as a success rate differential of about 43% versus 56%. Since the criterion contrast constructed in this example was judged to be moderately large, these results tell the researcher something about what effect size would constitute an impressive treatment effect on the measure of interest. Thus we see that, using this measure, we are likely to be looking for treatment effects that will be .26 standard deviation units or smaller but nonetheless of potentially practical significance.

This example illustrates the ability of the criterion contrast approach to provide information about the relation between statistical effect size indicators such as ES and practical effects that are very specific to the particular samples, variables, and settings of a given treatment domain. Additionally, useful pilot information is provided on such important features of the research situation as the variability of the samples of interest on candidate dependent variables which will aid in the design of subsequent treatment effectiveness research.

Other Approaches

There are, of course, other approaches to prospective and retrospective assessment of effect size in addition to the three discussed here. A useful review of a variety of strategies is provided by Sechrest and Yeaton (1981). Among their suggestions are several with distinct advantages for certain circumstances that may occur in treatment effectiveness research.

In some practical situations, for example, it may be possible to quantify in monetary terms the cost of providing treatment and the benefits of its effects. Such cost-benefit studies, when feasible, bear directly on the question of what effect size is meaningful. One answer is that the minimal effect worth achieving and, for research purposes, worth detecting is that for which the value of its benefits at least equals the cost of producing those benefits.

Another circumstance that lends itself to a distinctive strategy is one in which the treatment effects of interest should have overt behavioral manifestations. For instance, we would expect a stutterer benefiting from speech therapy to stutter noticeably less in everyday situations. In such cases, the "just-noticeable-difference" approach might be used. The criterion for a minimal meaningful effect size would be set at the interval on an appropriate measure corresponding to the least improvement that family, friends, and associates would notice in ordinary conversations with a subject.

In many research contexts, however, determining the minimal, meaningful effect size will be a judgment call not readily defended by reference to norms, criterion groups, cost-benefit analysis, and the like. In such cases, Sechrest and Yeaton suggest that the researcher's intuition at least be supplemented by the judgment of experts in the treatment area at issue. For example, using the statistical translation approach described earlier, a range of effect sizes on a given dependent variable might be presented in the relatively comprehensible form of, say, success rate differentials. Various appropriate experts could then be asked what size effects might be expected from a given treatment and what minimal size would be of practical significance. With the distribution of experts' judgments in hand, the researcher is in a stronger position for setting a minimal effect size to detect in research on the treatment of interest and for assessing the results actually obtained in such research.

Summary

Designing treatment effectiveness research that meets some adequate standard of statistical power requires the researcher to have a rather specific numerical value for the minimal effect size believed worth detecting. In cases where that value is not already established prior to planning the research, this chapter recommends that some systematic approach to determining that value be adopted as part of the planning process. Among the general approaches that can be used are: 1) selecting a reasonable value from the distribution of effects found by other researchers in similar studies (actuarial approach); 2) setting a value in practical terms easy to judge, such as success rate differences between experimental groups, and converting that value into the equivalent *ES* value (statistical translation approach); and 3) basing the value on the *ES* equivalent of the contrast between two nonexperimental groups recognized to differ in practical terms on the variable of interest (criterion group contrast approach). Other more specialized approaches can be used when circumstances permit.

Whatever the approach used, the message of this chapter is that the effect size is an elusive and ambiguous parameter in treatment effectiveness research. A researcher who does not know with some degree of precision what he or she is looking for, nor how to assess the practical significance of what is found, is entering a murky world in which largely inappropriate statistical conventions replace reasoned judgment. The result, all too often, is grossly underpowered research so prone to inferential error that it is more likely to obscure the truth than to illuminate it.

4. How to Estimate Statistical Power

There are two approaches to actually determining numerical values for statistical power and the associated parameters. Like making a cake, it can be done "from scratch" based on statistical theory or "from a package" by looking up values on precomputed tables. As a practical matter it is easier to use precomputed tables, and we will follow that approach here. A particularly complete and usable reference work of statistical power tables is Jacob Cohen's (1977, 1988) *Statistical Power Analysis for the Behavioral Sciences*. It presents tables for a range of common statistical tests and provides instructions for using those tables under a variety of conditions and assumptions. Other useful general reference works along similar lines include Owen (1962, 1965), upon which Cohen relies in part, and Kraemer and Thiemann (1987). The reader should turn to works such as these for information on determining statistical power beyond that presented in this chapter.

A Generic Approach to the Power of Experimental Comparisons

In the remainder of this chapter we will not attempt to duplicate the breadth and detail of tabled information for determining statistical power that is in the reference literature mentioned above. Instead, a simple set of general charts will be provided for purposes of illustrating power relationships and for the convenience of the reader who wishes to do power analysis for the most common treatment effectiveness designs. These charts are based on the t-test and can be used with those statistical tests mathematically related to the t-test, a group which, fortunately, includes most of the common statistical tests used to compare experimental groups in treatment effectiveness research. These charts are restricted to the two-group comparison— for example, treatment versus control—that is the most common format for such research. In cases where a researcher plans to use multiple groups—for example, several treatment variations and/or several control groups—a partial power analysis can be done in this framework by selecting a key two-group comparison from among the various possibilities. Alternatively, the appropriate sections of Cohen (1977, 1988, especially chap. 8) or Kraemer and Thiemann (1987) can be used to conduct a full power analysis.

General procedure. The last section of this chapter contains a set of charts depicting the statistical power for various values of the effect size, the sample size, and the alpha level. Those charts are constructed around the generic effect size parameter, *ES*, which can represent the specific effect size parameters associated with t-tests, one-way analysis of variance and covariance ($k = 2$ samples), point-biserial correlation, 2×2 Chi-square, and tests of the difference between proportions.

The first step in using those charts is to determine the statistical test appropriate to significance testing and the corresponding formulation of the effect size parameter that makes the charts applicable. There are instructions for each statistical test preceding the charts.

The second step is to enter the charts with any three of the relevant parameters and determine the fourth. For example, one could enter the charts with a given effect size, sample size, and alpha and determine the corresponding statistical power. It is also possible to set a desired level of statistical power, then enter the charts with the effect size and alpha to determine the sample size necessary to attain that power. Alternatively, one might determine the minimal effect size that can be detected at a given power using a given sample size and alpha, or the alpha at which a given power is attained for a given effect size and sample size.

The use of charts instead of tables for these purposes is intended to aid the reader in getting an overview of the nature of the relationships among the various parameters involved in statistical power. It is much easier to comprehend those relationships when they are presented in graphical form than in a table of numbers. The advantage of tables, of course, is that the values can be specified more precisely than can be obtained from the charts even with the most careful application of ruler and magnifying glass. Nonetheless, the charts are serviceable for practical purposes. Treatment effectiveness research has an inherent disorderliness that argues against an attempt to estimate statistical power, effect size, and so forth to the *n*th decimal place. The reader who requires more exact values than can be extracted from the charts in this chapter should consult the reference works cited earlier.

An illustration. Before getting to the detailed charts that are designed to permit fairly close determination of power values, it is instructive to look at a somewhat cruder chart of power relations to get an idea of their nature and the various ways in which such a chart can be used. Figure 4.1 shows the functions relating sample size to power for various values of the effect size, assuming a t-test comparison between two experimental groups and alpha = .05. Sample size refers to the number of subjects in *each* group—for example, 10 treatment subjects compared with 10 control subjects is represented as a sample size of 10. Effect size is represented as *ES* values, the difference between the means of the treatment group and control group in standard deviation units.

There are several interesting features of Figure 4.1. The relationship between power and sample size, for example, is noteworthy since many textbooks treat statistical power primarily in terms of determining appropriate sample size. Figure 4.1 shows an asymptotic relationship—with increased numbers of subjects each power curve generally increases rapidly until it begins to flatten out near the limit of power = 1.00. Thus power increases much more sharply when additional subjects are added to smaller samples—for example, *n* less than 200—than when the same number is added to larger samples.

Equally interesting is the relationship between effect size and statistical power for a given sample size. At any given sample size below about 200, statistical power increases dramatically with increases in effect size. To examine better the shape of this relationship, the reader should select a sample size in that range and inspect the intervals between the successive *ES* curves. Generally, the intervals are longer in the middle and lower portion of the *ES* range and much shorter in the upper portion of that range. This means that under most practical circumstances altering a small or medium effect size will change power more than altering a large effect size. An important key to designing sensitive treatment effectiveness research is to recognize that effect size can often be altered. Part II of this volume discusses various ways to increase the operative effect size in a study.

The joint influence of effect size and sample size on statistical power is perhaps the most important relationship to be understood from Figure 4.1. If we want to detect treatment effects, when present, with high probability, say 90–95% as suggested earlier in this volume, great practical difficulty ensues. Figure 4.1 shows that, for small to modest sample size, this power level is attained only for relatively large effect sizes, *ES* in the range of .60 and above. As shown in Chapter 3 from meta-analysis results, *ES* in treat-

72

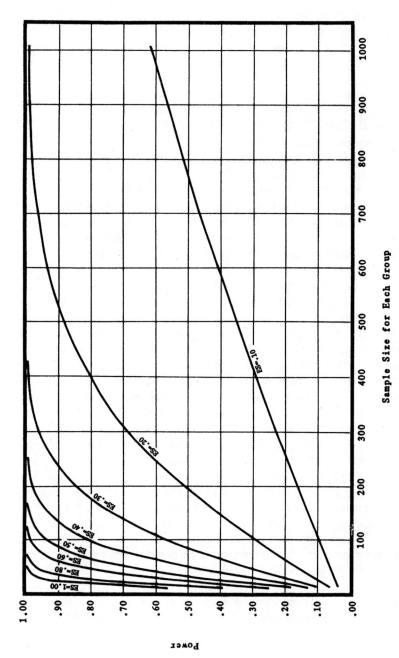

Figure 4.1: Power as a Function of Sample Size and Effect Size for $\alpha = .05$

ment effectiveness research is quite often below .60. If we wish to detect smaller effects with high power, we must have rather large samples—for example, over 250–300 in *each* experimental group for $ES = .30$ and well over 500 for $ES = .20$. For $ES = .10$, even a sample of 1000 is insufficient. Such samples are much larger than are often used in treatment effectiveness research and, indeed, are larger than can be realistically attained in many research settings. The practical dilemma for the researcher, therefore, is that under ordinary circumstances research will often either be limited to detecting only rather large treatment effects or will require larger samples than are available.

For purposes of planning and assessing treatment effectiveness research, it may be advisable for the researcher to make a systematic examination of statistical power as a function of each of the other relevant parameters. In this way a determination can be made not only of whether there is adequate power but also of how the power would change if any of the parameters were changed. One useful way to depict these relationships is to make separate plots showing power over the practical range of one parameter while the other two are fixed. The values needed to construct such plots can be readily extracted from the power charts included at the end of this chapter. The technique is easier to demonstrate than to describe, however, so we will illustrate using a hypothetical "typical" experiment.

First, we set the values of the various power parameters that we expect to have (or in fact have) in the experiment of interest and determine the range over which they might be realistically varied given the constraints on the research situation. For our hypothetical typical treatment effectiveness experiment, we can set alpha at the conventional level of .05 and assume that it might be permissible to have it vary from .01 to, say, .20 without provoking cries of outrage from the research community. From the distributions of meta-analysis results presented in Chapter 3, we found that the median effect size for treatment effectiveness research was about $ES = .40$ with the preponderance of values falling between zero and 1.00. To identify typical sample size values, we turn to Lipsey et al. (1985) who reported descriptive information about a random sample of 122 published treatment effectiveness studies. They found a median sample size of about 40 with approximately 80% of the distribution falling between $n = 10$ and $n = 200$.

If we determine the statistical power of our typical study from Figure 4.1 or Figure 4.4 (at the end of this chapter) the result is disappointing—for alpha $= .05$, $ES = .40$, and $n = 40$, power is only .42. We conclude that the typical study is woefully underpowered, indeed, has less than a 50% chance of detecting the expected treatment effect. The question for the moment, however, is how the power would change with various alterations of sample size, effect size, and alpha. We can depict those relationships in three graphs: one each showing power as a function of alpha, sample size, or effect size while the other two parameters are kept fixed. If we plot each relationship over the selected range and use the same size graph for each, we can get a good visual comparison among them. Figure 4.2 shows such a set of plots for the hypothetical experiment described, but a similar set could be made for any range of variation in alpha, *ES*, and *n* in which a researcher was interested.

Comparison of the three plots in Figure 4.2 tells us a lot about the circumstances of our hypothetical research study. First, we see that changes in alpha, the easiest parameter to alter since it is set by the researcher, produces relatively modest changes in power. Changes in sample size or effect size, on the other hand, are capable of producing much more dramatic changes. Moreover, over the typical range of variation, increases in *ES* and proportionate increases in *n* are about equally effective in increasing power.

Where the curves cross the line for the desired criterion power level, they indicate a combination of parameters that will produce adequate power. The dotted line on each plot, for example, identifies the parameter values for which a power level of .95 is attained. With this information the researcher is in a position to analyze how to ensure adequate power in a particular study. As Figure 4.2 shows, our hypothetical study would attain a .95 power criterion if sample size were increased to 160 in each experimental group or, alternatively, if effect size were increased to .85. No increase in alpha within the plotted range, however, is sufficient to reach that criterion.

Further analysis along these lines might examine combinations of changes in the parameters. Turning back to Figure 4.1 (or forward to Figure 4.4), for example, we see that .95 power at $\alpha = .05$ could be attained by increasing sample size from 40 to 80 *and ES* from .40 to .60. Coupled with a practical assessment of the cost and effort required to alter sample size, effect size, and alpha, such an analysis permits a researcher to consider the most efficient means of attaining adequate statistical power in a study.

Before leaving Figure 4.2, we should note the implications of the various plots for the possible downhill slide of statistical power. Our typical study hypothesized a sample size of 40, an effect size of .40, and an alpha of .05. What happens to statistical power if each of these parameters is degraded below the levels hypothesized. As Figure 4.2 shows, power erodes very dramatically as the effect size is decreased over the likely

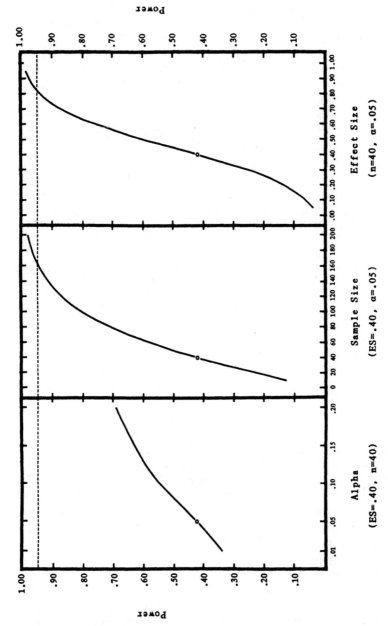

Figure 4.2: Changes in Power with Changes in α, *n*, and *ES* for a "Typical" Study (α = .05, *n* = 40, *ES* = .40)

range, somewhat less so but still substantially with decreases of sample size, and much less so with decreases in alpha. In planning for experimental control and procedures to maintain the integrity of the experiment, therefore, the researcher has the greatest downside risk if the effect size deteriorates—for example, via incomplete or inconsistent application of treatment, unreliable measures, excessive sample heterogeneity, and so forth. Erosion of sample size—for example, via attrition—also clearly presents problems that it would be desirable to prevent. Since some erosion in *both* these factors can be expected in most practical treatment effectiveness research, a wise strategy is to design for greater statistical power than the acceptable minimum and calculate the amount of erosion in the critical factors that can be permitted before the power slides below that minimum. For example, a researcher dealing with our hypothetical circumstances might design the study with a sample size of 180 and explicitly recognize that if, when implemented, the *n* falls below 160 in each group the power will drop under the criterion power level of .95.

Using the Power Charts

The charts at the end of this chapter are built on the same model as Figure 4.1. Statistical power is plotted on the vertical axis and sample size on the horizontal axis. Separate curves on the plot present the power function for each of a range of effect size values. Each chart depicts the relationships at a given alpha level; for a different alpha, a different chart must be used. Unlike Figure 4.1, these charts are plotted on "sideways" log-log paper which makes it easier to determine numerical values in the lower range of sample size and the upper range of effect size where the power curves are otherwise close together and difficult to read.

To use these charts, the researcher must first decide which significance test is appropriate for the research under consideration and turn to the discussion of that test in the next section of this chapter. Appearing there will be information about how the effect size parameter is handled for that particular statistical test. Additional comments will indicate any particular issues that apply to sample size and alpha for that test. It should be noted that, to be used properly, each of these statistical tests requires that certain specific assumptions be met, as described in any basic text on statistical analysis (e.g., Hays, 1973; Kirk, 1982).

Unless otherwise indicated, sample size and alpha are handled as follows for all the statistical tests:

Sample size. Sample size refers throughout to the number of subjects in *each* experimental group. Thus if 20 subjects in the treatment condition are compared to 20 subjects in the control condition, the sample size is 20, *not* 40. The power charts therefore assume that there will be equal numbers of subjects in each condition. When the number of subjects is not equal, the researcher should follow the advice of Cohen (1977) and compute the harmonic mean of n_t and n_c as follows:

$$n' = \frac{2n_t n_c}{n_t + n_c}$$

Using the power charts with the harmonic mean for unequal sample sizes will be relatively accurate when the larger n is no more than twice the smaller n or when the resulting n' is greater than 25 (Cohen, 1977, p. 42).

Alpha. Each power chart depicts power curves for a different alpha level, ranging from .01 to .20. Though $\alpha = .20$ is higher than is conventionally used for significance testing, it is presented here because treatment effectiveness researchers may sometimes find themselves in situations where alpha must be relaxed beyond the usual conventions in order to maintain some reasonable balance between the probabilities of Type I and Type II error. Both two-tailed significance testing (treatment either better or worse than control) and one-tailed testing (treatment only better than control, or only worse, but not both) are accommodated in the charts. The numerical relations are the same for a two-tailed test at a given alpha as for a one-tailed test at half that alpha, and both values appear on each chart.

The Statistical Tests

The t-test or One-Way ANOVA for Two Independent Samples

Perhaps the most common significance test for two-group comparisons in treatment effectiveness research is the t-test for independent samples. It applies where the independent variable is a categorical index of group membership (e.g., treatment group vs. control group) and the dependent variable is graduated, that is, it has values that range along some continuum. Completely equivalent is the one-way fixed effects analysis of variance (ANOVA) with $k = 2$ groups. Indeed, as is well-known, under these circumstances the t-test value and the F-test value from ANOVA are related as $t = \sqrt{F}$.

For the general case of the t-test or one-way ANOVA applied to compare two independent samples of subjects, the effect size with which to enter the power charts is the difference between the means divided by the within-group standard deviation, that is, the same *ES* index used to illustrate effect size in previous portions of this volume. This index is defined as:

$$ES_{ai} = \frac{\mu_t - \mu_c}{\sigma} \qquad [A]$$

Where ES_{ai} is the effect size formulation to use in the power charts for the t-test or ANOVA between two independent samples; μ_t and μ_c are the means of the treatment and control populations respectively; and σ is the common standard deviation of the two populations.

While *ES* is defined here in terms of population values, for practical purposes μ_t, μ_c, and σ are generally estimated from sample data. The absolute value of the *ES* expression is used to enter the power charts though, for descriptive purposes, the convention is to use positive *ES* values to mean that the treatment group is "superior" to the control group on the pertinent dependent variable and negative values to indicate control group superiority.

The common standard deviation used in the denominator of the *ES* expression can be estimated by pooling the estimates derived from sample data (s_t and s_c). Pooling is accomplished by weighting by sample size as follows:

$$\text{For } n_t \neq n_c \qquad s_p = \sqrt{\frac{(n_t - 1)s_t^2 + (n_c - 1)s_c^2}{(n_t - 1) + (n_c - 1)}} \qquad [B]$$

$$\text{For } n_t = n_c \qquad s_p = \sqrt{\frac{s_t^2 + s_c^2}{2}} \qquad [C]$$

Where s_p is the pooled standard deviation; s_t^2 and s_c^2 are the variances for the treatment and control group respectively; and n_t and n_c are the sample sizes for the treatment and control groups.

It should be noted that if n_t and n_c are not equal *and* σ_t and σ_c are not equal, the *ES* values constructed with the various formulas given above for averaging *n* and estimating σ will not yield correct power functions from the charts. Small inequalities may produce negligible distortion for practical purposes; larger ones, however, could lead to serious misestimates of power. In such cases, power can be estimated as a range bracketed by two separate estimates, one assuming the *n* and σ (or *s*) of the treatment group and the other assuming the *n* and σ (or *s*) of the control group.

Example. A researcher planning a study of the effects of preoperative counseling on the rate of recovery for elective surgery patients decides that her study should be able to detect an *ES* as small as .30 with 90% power using a t-test for independent samples and $\alpha = .05$. Examining the power chart in Figure 4.4 she discovers that the *ES* = .30 curve crosses the Power = .90 line at about $n = 235$. She concludes that her study must have at least 235 subjects in the treatment group and an equal number in the control group.

Alternatively, this same researcher may determine that the maximum number of subjects she will be able to obtain for the treatment and control groups will be 100 in each. Again consulting Figure 4.4, she finds that the $n = 100$ line crosses the Power = .90 line at a point between the *ES* = .45 and *ES* = .50 curves. By interpolation she concludes that, using a t-test and $\alpha = .05$, her study will attain the desired power only for *ES* equal to or larger than about .46.

Additionally, in examining the literature, this researcher finds that the best previous study of this intervention used $n = 50$ in each experimental group. From the reported sample means and standard deviations for the treatment and control groups in that study she calculates the *ES* found there using equations [A] and [B] above. This results in an *ES* estimate of .25. Consulting Figure 4.4 she notes that the $n = 50$ line crosses the *ES* = .25 curve at a power of about .24. She is thus not surprised that this study found no statistically significant difference between the treatment and control group using a t-test and $\alpha = .05$.

The t-test for Dependent (Correlated) Samples or the One-Way ANOVA with Paired Observations (k = 2 Samples)

An important variant on the t-test and one-way ANOVA is the case where the two samples being compared are not independent but, instead, consist of observations that are paired in some way such that the members of each pair are more similar than the members of different pairs. The most familiar case is the pre-post or repeated measures design in which each subject "serves as his/her own control." Each pair of observations thus consists of the value of the dependent variable at Time 1 (pretreatment) and the value at Time 2 (posttreatment) for a particular subject. An analogous case occurs when two different subjects are represented in each pair but, prior to the experiment, they are matched on some relevant characteristic or set of characteristics. One subject from each pair is then assigned to the treatment group and the other to the control group. To the extent that the chosen matching variables are related to the dependent variable at issue, subjects within these pairs will have more similar values on the dependent variable than unpaired subjects. These designs and their advantages for variance control are discussed more fully in Chapter 6.

In both these cases, the net result is that the t-test or F-test is based on a sampling error estimate or "error term" that is reduced in proportion to the strength of the correlation (r_{tc}) between the paired values (assuming, as is likely, that the correlation is positive). Correspondingly, the denominator of the ES effect size index decreases and the operative effect size increases. In particular, whereas in the uncorrelated case the denominator of ES was σ, the common standard deviation, in the correlated case the denominator is $\sigma\sqrt{(1 - r_{tc})}$. This formula can be used to produce ES for paired observations as follows:

$$ES_{ap} = \frac{\mu_t - \mu_c}{\sigma\sqrt{1 - r_{tc}}} = \frac{ES_{ai}}{\sqrt{1 - r_{tc}}} \qquad [D]$$

Where ES_{ap} is the effect size formulation for the correlated t-test or one-way ANOVA with paired observations; μ_t and μ_c are the means for the treatment and control populations respectively; σ is the common standard deviation of the two populations; r_{tc} is the correlation between the paired values in those populations; and ES_{ai} is the effect size formulation for the analogous t-test or ANOVA between independent samples.

Note that there is some loss of degrees of freedom for the correlated t-test and ANOVA with paired observations relative to the independent samples versions. For the correlated case, $df = n - 1$, while for independent samples $df = 2n - 2$. Thus the critical t-value or F-value required to attain statistical significance is somewhat larger for the correlated or repeated measures case, though the difference is negligible for $n > 15$. The power charts at the end of this chapter assume independent samples; in cases of very small n the researcher may need to make some adjustment—for example, using a table for a more stringent alpha level.

Example. A researcher is planning a study to compare an innovative "cooperative learning" curriculum with conventional instruction for teaching mathematics to underachieving fourth graders. A standardized mathematics achievement test that is annually administered to all fourth graders is chosen as the outcome variable. One-half a grade year equivalent on that test is chosen as the minimal effect of practical significance, that is, the amount by which the new curriculum should outperform the old one. Using the test norms, the researcher determines that the average increase from fourth to fifth grade is 20 points and the standard deviation of scores is 50. The minimal *ES* to be detected, therefore, is .20 (10/50).

Recognizing that an *ES* of .20 cannot be reliably detected in an independent samples comparison without a group *n* of about 500, which exceeds available students, the researcher chooses to pair subjects according to their third grade scores on the achievement test of interest and then randomly assign one student from each pair to the new curriculum and the other to the old. Since third-grade scores have proven to be strong predictors of fourth-grade scores, he estimates that the correlation between these pairs on their fourth-grade scores will be at least .85. With this design, using equation [D] above, the operative *ES* is increased from .20 to .20/$\sqrt{1 - .85}$ = .52. Figure 4.4 shows that an *ES* = .50 or greater can be detected with a power of .95 at α = .05 with a group *n* of about 110, that is, 220 subjects total, assembled into 110 pairs.

ANOVA with a Blocking Factor (k = 2 Samples)

In this design subjects are first categorized into blocks, that is, groups of subjects that are similar to each other on some characteristic related to the dependent measure. For example, to use gender as a blocking variable, subjects would first be divided into males and females, then some males assigned to the treatment group and the rest to the control group and, separately, some females assigned to treatment and the rest to control. This design is like the paired observations design described above except that instead of each pair of observations constituting a "block" all by itself, there are a number of similar observations in the block. Also like the paired observation design, it has advantages for variance control and is discussed more fully in Chapter 6.

In either the paired observations or blocked case, the overall variance on the dependent measure can be viewed as the sum of two components: the within-blocks variance and the between-blocks variance. The efficiency of this design is gained because it removes the contribution of the between-blocks variance to the error term against which effects are tested. Correspondingly, the denominator of the *ES* is reduced and the operative *ES* is increased. Thus if the total variance were $\sigma^2 = \sigma_b^2 + \sigma_w^2$, encompassing both between- and within-blocks variance, we wish to use only σ_w^2 as the variability relevant for testing statistical significance, that is, remove σ_b^2 from the total. If we let PV_b equal the proportion of the variance represented by the differences among blocks, the researcher can calculate *ES* for this case on the assumption of independent (uncorrelated, unblocked) samples using the techniques described earlier for the independent sample t-test and then adjust the result to represent the role of the blocking factor as follows:

$$ES_{ab} = \frac{\mu_t - \mu_c}{\sigma_w} = \frac{\mu_t - \mu_c}{\sigma\sqrt{1 - PV_b}} = \frac{ES_{ai}}{\sqrt{1 - PV_b}} \qquad [E]$$

Where ES_{ab} is the effect size formulation for the blocked one-way analysis of variance; ES_{ai} is the effect size formulation for the analogous unblocked one-way ANOVA; PV_b is σ_b^2/σ^2 where σ_b^2 is the between-blocks variance and σ^2 is the common variance of the treatment and control populations.

The researcher, therefore, can estimate PV_b, the between-blocks variance as a proportion of the common (or pooled) variance within experimental groups, and use it to adjust the effect size estimate in such a way as to allow the power charts at the end of this chapter to be used in the usual way (see Chapter 6 for alternate forms of PV_b). The degrees of freedom will be reduced by one less than the number of blocks formed, but this will generally have little influence on power unless the number of blocks is large relative to the sample size.

Example. A sports psychologist is investigating the effects of mental practice on the performance of college athletes, specifically whether mental rehearsal beforehand improves runners' times in a 400-meter race. Since fractions of a second can be important in a competitive race, she wishes to detect an effect as small as three-tenths of a second. Using practice times for the men and women on the varsity track team, she estimates the standard deviation of their times in the 400-meter run to be about 2.00 seconds ($s^2 = 4.00$). The minimal ES of interest, therefore, is determined to be .15, that is, .3/2.00. Being interested only in improved performance and recognizing that it is difficult to detect such small effects, the researcher selects a one-tailed test and sets a fairly liberal alpha of .10 before consulting Figure 4.7 to determine the sample size needed to attain a power of .80. The required n for each group turns out to be about 400 (800 total), far more subjects than are available in the local setting.

On closer inspection of the data for the practice times, however, the researcher realizes that most of the variance is due to differences between the times for men and those for women. Blocking the data by sex produces a standard deviation of about .75 within each group ($s_w^2 = .56$) with the remainder of the variance being between groups ($s_b^2 = 3.44$). That is, 86% of the total variance was between blocks (3.44/4.00). Adjusting the ES variance term to remove the between-blocks component, as in equation [E] above, three-tenths of a second corresponds to an *ES* of .40 (i.e., .3/.75 or .3/2$\sqrt{1 - .86}$). Again consulting Figure 4.7, the researcher discovers that at $\alpha = .10$, one-tailed, a power of .80 can be attained for *ES* = .40 with a sample of about 60 in each experimental group. She therefore designs the study as an ANOVA with subjects blocked by gender, 30 female and 30 male runners in the treatment group and 30 females and 30 males in the control group.

Analysis of Covariance (k = 2 Samples)

Another useful variation on the t-test or analogous one-way ANOVA is to adjust the variance of the dependent measure scores by removing the influence of a covariate. This procedure would usually be conducted as a one-way analysis of covariance (ANCOVA) or as a semipartial correlation between the independent variable and the dependent variable with the covariate variable partialed out from the dependent variable but not from the independent variable. For example, a researcher with a reading achievement test as a dependent variable may wish to remove the component of performance related to IQ before comparing the treatment and control groups. This design is discussed in more detail in Chapter 6 along with the other variance control designs.

To the extent that the covariate is correlated with the dependent variable, this procedure reduces the sampling error estimate proportionately. The denominator of the effect size index is correspondingly smaller, the operative *ES* is larger, and statistical power is greater. This relationship can be expressed as follows, where r_{dc} is the correlation between the dependent variable and the covariate across both experimental groups:

$$ES_{ac} = \frac{\mu_t - \mu_c}{\sigma\sqrt{1 - r_{dc}^2}} = \frac{ES_{ai}}{\sqrt{1 - r_{dc}^2}} \qquad [F]$$

Where ES_{ac} is the effect size formulation for the one-way analysis of covariance; μ_t and μ_c are the means for the treatment and control populations respectively; σ is the common standard deviation; and r_{dc} is the correlation between the dependent variable and the covariate.

For this variant on the t-test and one-way ANOVA, the power charts can be used with ES_{ac} to give good estimates of power. Note, however, that the degrees of freedom for the significance test are reduced by one for each covariate used in this procedure. Unless the sample size is very small or the number of covariates is large, however, this should have little effect on the power relationship.

Example. A researcher is planning a study to investigate whether a new computer workstation improves the productivity of the personnel who process claims forms in a large insurance company. The outcome variable of interest is the number of cases completed per week. Based on the cost of the workstations, management estimates that at least a 20% increase in productivity is required for the workstations to be cost effective. Productivity data from prior months indicates that the average worker completes about 50 cases per week, but individual performance ranges from about 20 cases to over 70 (standard deviation, 13.3). From this data, the researcher determines that a 20% average productivity increase is equivalent to an *ES* of .75. Figure 4.4 shows that, at $\alpha = .05$, a power of .90 could be attained for *ES* = .75 with about 40 subjects in each experimental group. Because of the expense of leasing workstations for research purposes, however, the researcher wishes to make the experiment more efficient. He determines that the average correlation between the workers' productivity in one month and that in the subsequent month is .80, indicating stable individual differences among workers in their level of performance. Introducing prior productivity level into the study as a covariate, using equation [F] above, increases the operative *ES* from .75 to 1.25, that is, $.75/\sqrt{1 - .80^2}$. Figure 4.4 shows that this design has a power of .90 at $\alpha = .05$ with only about 15 subjects in each experimental group.

Correlation and Multiple Regression

Though relatively uncommon, treatment effectiveness can be tested in terms of correlation coefficients. For instance, point biserial correlation (r_{pb}) can be used to test the relationship between a dichotomous independent variable (e.g., 0 vs. 1) representing group membership (e.g., control vs. treatment) and a graduated dependent variable of interest. Power estimation can proceed through conversion of the relevant value of the correlation coefficient into the *ES* index as follows:

$$ES_r = \frac{r_{pb}}{\sqrt{pq\,(1 - r_{pb}^2)}} \text{ or,}$$

$$\text{for equal } n \ (p = q = .5), \ ES_r = \frac{2r_{pb}}{\sqrt{1 - r_{pb}^2}}$$

[G]

Where ES_r is the effect size formulation for the correlation; r_{pb} is the point-biserial correlation to be converted to *ES*; and *p* and *q*, respectively, are the proportions of the total sample in the treatment group and the control group $(p+q=1)$.

Use of the power charts involves only entering with ES_r as the effect size. Note, however, that the n in the charts, sample size for one experimental group, is *half* the N over which the correlation is computed in the case of equal sized groups and is $2n_t n_c/(n_t + n_c)$ for unequal-sized groups, as in the corresponding t-test formulation.

Where one or more covariate variables are involved, as well as the independent variable and the dependent variable, treatment effects can be tested as the semipartial correlation coefficient (the independent variable-dependent variable correlation with the covariate variable or linear combination of covariate variables partialed out from the dependent variable) or in multiple regression format. In the latter case, a hierarchical multiple regression is used with the covariate variable entered first, then the independent variable, with treatment effects tested by determining if the independent variable contributes significantly to accounting for dependent variable variance beyond that accounted for by the covariate variable (Cohen & Cohen, 1975).

Where the independent variable-covariate variable correlation is zero or negligible, as when subjects are randomly assigned to treatment and control groups or are otherwise equivalent on the covariate variable, partial correlation and hierarchical multiple regression for testing treatment effects are equivalent to the analysis of covariance described earlier. Therefore, the ES can be adjusted for the role of the covariate as follows:

$$ES_{mr} = \frac{ES_r}{\sqrt{1 - r_{dc}^2}} \qquad \text{[H]}$$

Where ES_{mr} is the effect size formulation for multiple regression or partial correlation; ES_r is the effect size for the correlation between dependent and independent variables ignoring the covariate variables; and r_{dc} is the correlation of the dependent variable with the covariate or with a linear combination of covariates including those entered into multiple regression analysis prior to the independent variable.

Example. A researcher is investigating the relationship between participation in a cigarette smoking reduction program and number of cigarettes smoked in the month subsequent to the program. She wishes to design a study with a power of .90 and $\alpha = .01$ for any relationships between the independent variable and dependent variable as large as $r = .20$. Using equation [G] above, she determines that the equivalent ES for a comparison between two equal n experimental groups is .41, that is, $2(.2)/\sqrt{1 - .2^2}$. Figure 4.3 shows that for $ES = .41$, $\alpha = .01$, and Power $= .90$, a sample size of about 145 subjects in each experimental group is required. The researcher knows, however, that previous research has shown that the number of prior attempts to stop smoking is a moderate predictor $(r = .30)$ of success in treatment. If this variable is partialed out of the relationship between participation in treatment and subsequent smoking, the operative ES will increase to .43 (i.e., $.41/\sqrt{1 - .3^2}$, using equation [H] above). In this case, for the same alpha and power, Figure 4.3 shows that about 130 subjects in each experimental group will be sufficient, a modest savings.

Chi-Square and the Difference between Proportions

When dependent variables in treatment effectiveness research are categorical rather than continuous, the results are usually presented as a contingency table and tested using Chi-square or some test of the difference between proportions. A typical case, and the only one considered here, is the 2×2 contingency table in which the degree of association between a dichotomous group variable (e.g., treatment vs. control) and a dichotomous dependent variable (e.g., success vs. failure) is tested. Each cell of that table contains a frequency value, that is, the number of subjects in the indicated group with the indicated outcome.

For example, a researcher with 100 subjects evenly divided between treatment and control group and measured on a dependent variable with a "success" baserate of 50% would expect the following results under the null hypothesis:

	Success	Failure
Treatment	25	25
Control	25	25

A treatment effect that altered the success rate to 70% would produce the following table:

	Success	Failure
Treatment	35	15
Control	25	25

To do statistical power analysis for such a situation using the charts in this chapter, the data from the contingency table should first be converted to proportions within each experimental group. That is, the treatment group data should be represented as the proportion in each of the two outcome categories and the control data should be represented likewise. Thus the data for the above example would appear as:

	Success	Failure
Treatment	.70	.30
Control	.50	.50

Power relationships for the situation above can be determined to a close approximation using an effect size index based on the difference between the "success" proportions of the treatment versus control group (or whatever other category of interest is analogous to the success category of the example here). To compute the appropriate effect size, the relevant proportions must be transformed. Cohen (1977) uses the arcsine transformation as follows:

Let p_t be the success proportion for the treatment group;
let p_c be the analogous proportion for the control group;
Let ϕ_t be the arcsine transformation $2\arcsin(\sqrt{p_t})$ and correspondingly, $\phi_c = 2\arcsin(\sqrt{p_c})$.

The effect size index for the difference between p_t and p_c can then be expressed as follows:

$$ES_p = \phi_t - \phi_c \qquad [I]$$

Where ES_p is the effect size formulation for the difference between proportions, and ϕ_t and ϕ_c are the arcsine transformations of the success proportions for the treatment and control populations respectively.

Following convention, we assign ES_p the absolute value of the difference for purposes of determining power, then give it a plus sign if the treatment group results are superior to the control group results, a minus sign if the control group results are superior. Table 4.1 provides the arcsine transformations for proportions from .01 to .99 in increments of .01.

Example. Suppose a medical researcher is considering a study of a new cancer therapy in which the control group survival rate after two years is

TABLE 4.1 Arcsine Transformations (φ) for Proportions (p)

p	φ	p	φ	p	φ	p	φ
.01	.200	.26	1.070	.51	1.591	.76	2.118
.02	.284	.27	1.093	.52	1.611	.77	2.141
.03	.348	.28	1.115	.53	1.631	.78	2.165
.04	.403	.29	1.137	.54	1.651	.79	2.190
.05	.451	.30	1.159	.55	1.671	.80	2.214
.06	.495	.31	1.181	.56	1.691	.81	2.240
.07	.536	.32	1.203	.57	1.711	.82	2.265
.08	.574	.33	1.224	.58	1.731	.83	2.292
.09	.609	.34	1.245	.59	1.752	.84	2.319
.10	.644	.35	1.266	.60	1.772	.85	2.346
.11	.676	.36	1.287	.61	1.793	.86	2.375
.12	.707	.37	1.308	.62	1.813	.87	2.404
.13	.738	.38	1.328	.63	1.834	.88	2.434
.14	.767	.39	1.349	.64	1.855	.89	2.465
.15	.795	.40	1.369	.65	1.875	.90	2.498
.16	.823	.41	1.390	.66	1.897	.91	2.532
.17	.850	.42	1.410	.67	1.918	.92	2.568
.18	.876	.43	1.430	.68	1.939	.93	2.606
.19	.902	.44	1.451	.69	1.961	.94	2.647
.20	.927	.45	1.471	.70	1.982	.95	2.691
.21	.952	.46	1.491	.71	2.004	.96	2.739
.22	.976	.47	1.511	.72	2.026	.97	2.793
.23	1.000	.48	1.531	.73	2.049	.98	2.858
.24	1.024	.49	1.551	.74	2.071	.99	2.941
.25	1.047	.50	1.571	.75	2.094		

SOURCE: Computer generated using Microsoft Basic functions

anticipated to be 25% and treatment is expected to improve that to 40%. From Table 4.1, the arcsine transform of .40 is 1.369 and that of .25 is 1.047. The simple difference of these values as per equation [I] above (i.e., $1.369 - 1.047$) gives the effect size, $ES_p = .32$ (rounded). If the researcher has available 100 subjects for each experimental group, Figure 4.5 shows that at $\alpha = .10$ the power for detecting $ES = .32$ will be about .72.

The Power Charts

The charts in this section are based on computer generated values using Cohen's (1988) formulation of the Dixon and Massey (1957) approximation for the power of the t-test. They will yield reasonably close values of statistical power (generally within ± .03 or less) for the significance tests discussed above. The reader should consult Cohen (1977, 1988) or Kraemer and Thiemann (1987) if more precision is desired. Each of the charts shows the relationships of power, generic effect size (*ES*), and sample size for a given alpha level. Thus to compare power for different alpha levels, one must move from chart to chart. Charts are presented for one-tailed and two-tailed alpha equal to .01, .05, .10, .15, and .20, the range within which most practical research will be conducted. Alpha is labeled first on each chart to represent bi-directional or two-tailed tests: that is, significance testing to reject the null hypothesis both when the treatment group results exceed those of the control group *and* when the control group results exceed those of the treatment group. For one-directional tests, that is, those in which only treatment group superiority (or inferiority) counts toward rejecting the null hypothesis, the charts can be used by assuming alpha equal to half the two-tailed value, also indicated on each chart. Thus the alpha = .10 chart for two-tailed significance tests also gives appropriate values for the case of one-tailed testing with alpha = .05.

Figures 4.3 to 4.9 follow on pp. 90 – 96

90

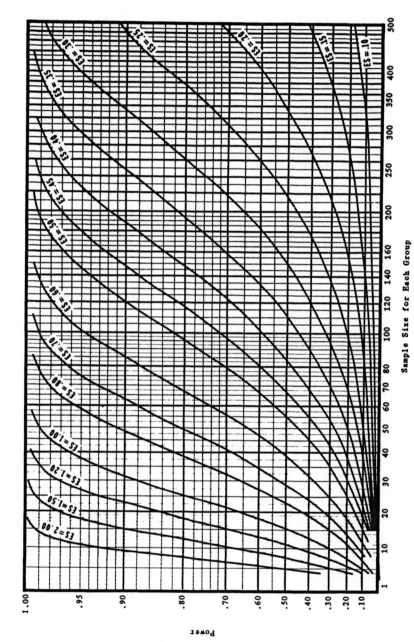

Figure 4.3: Power Chart for α = .01, Two-Tailed or α = .005, One-Tailed

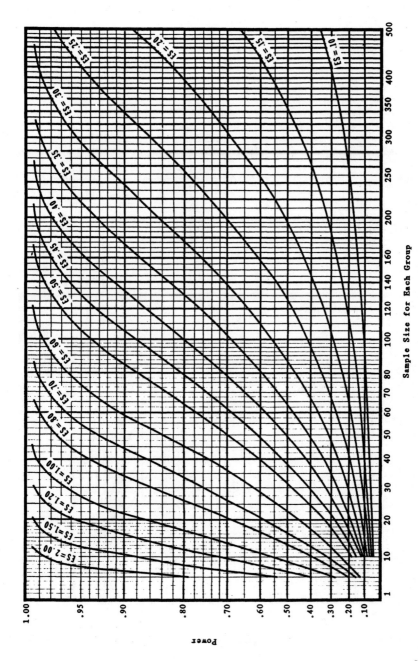

Figure 4.4: Power Chart for α = .05, Two-Tailed or α = .025, One-Tailed

91

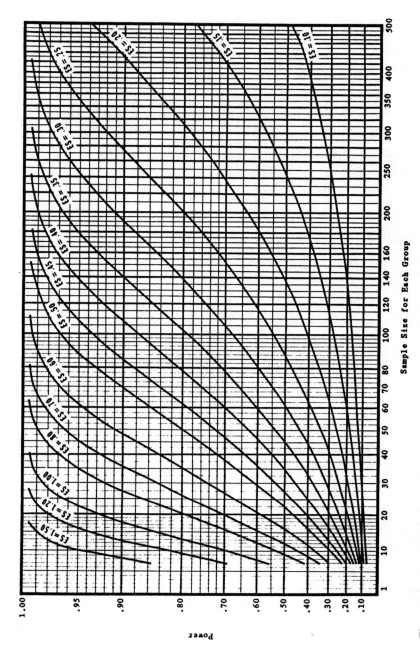

Figure 4.5: Power Chart for $\alpha = .10$, Two-Tailed or $\alpha = .05$, One-Tailed

92

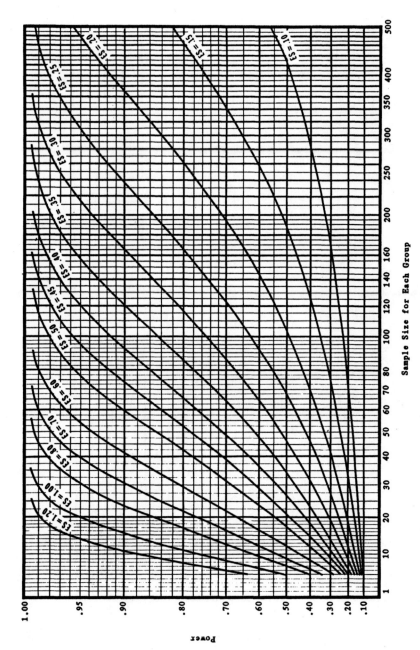

Figure 4.6: Power Chart for $\alpha = .15$, Two-Tailed or $\alpha = .075$, One-Tailed

93

94

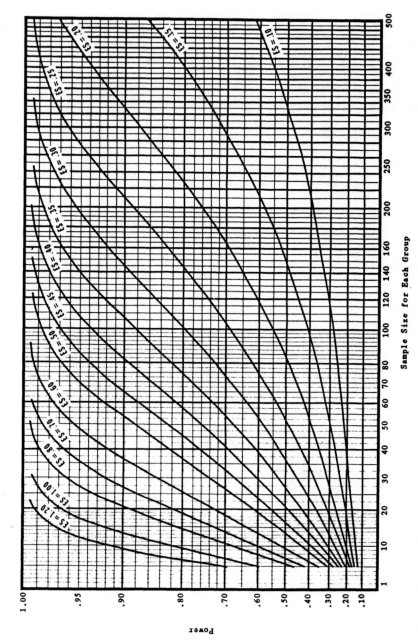

ES = .20
ES = .25
ES = .15
ES = .30
ES = .35
ES = .10
ES = .40
ES = .45
ES = .50
ES = .60
ES = .70
ES = .80
ES = 1.00
ES = 1.20

Power

Sample Size for Each Group

Figure 4.7: Power Chart for $\alpha = .20$, Two-Tailed or $\alpha = .10$, One-Tailed

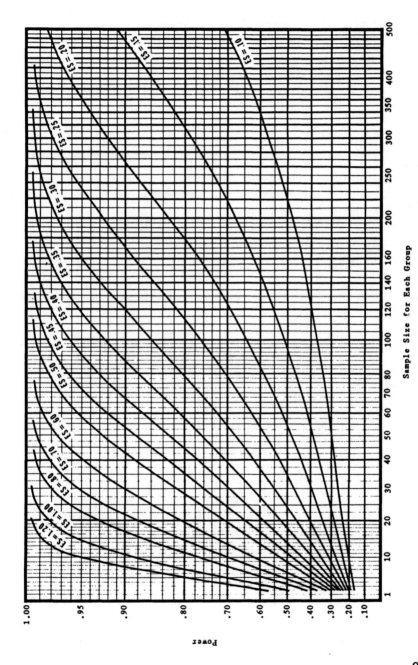

Figure 4.8: Power Chart for α = .30, Two-Tailed or α = .15, One-Tailed

95

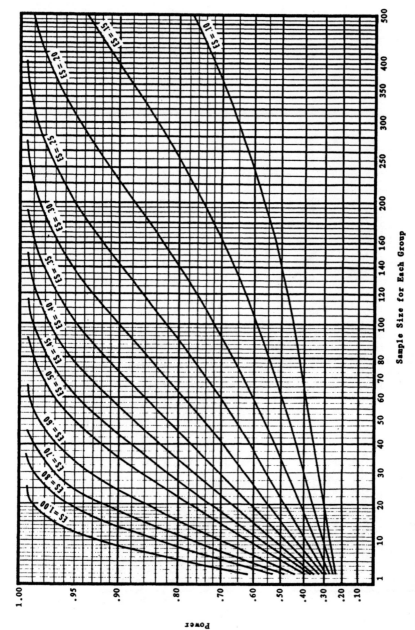

Figure 4.9: Power Chart for α = .40, Two-Tailed or α = .20, One-Tailed

Part II

Useful Approaches and Techniques

As argued in Part I of this volume, the researcher who wishes to detect treatment effects when they are present must design studies with adequate statistical power. Of the various factors that influence statistical power, attention usually centers on sample size. As the previous sections of this volume indicate, increasing sample size will increase power, all other things being equal. Determining the sample size necessary for a study to attain the desired level of statistical power is therefore an essential aspect of research planning. Unfortunately, it is not always possible to obtain the sample size dictated by such analysis. In such cases the researcher needs alternative approaches that will yield adequate statistical power or, at least, enhance statistical power without necessitating unrealistically large samples.

Moreover, even when there are ample numbers of subjects, large samples may not be the most efficient or cost-effective way in which to attain statistical power. Under most research circumstances there are very real costs associated with each subject included in a research design. The researcher must figure not only the cost of the research procedures, including the recruiting and maintenance of the subject pool, but the cost of monitoring and, in some cases, delivering the treatment and control procedures to each subject. Under these circumstances, the researcher would want to design the study so that the desired level of power was attained from the minimal number of subjects.

Part II of this volume focuses on the variety of factors a researcher should consider in planning research with adequate statistical power. Its emphasis is upon the ways in which power can be increased if the researcher is willing to plan the study carefully and undertake some preliminary or "pilot" tests of various features of the plan. Because they are generally so neglected in discussions of power, special emphasis is given to those ways in which power can be increased without depending solely upon the brute force of large samples. Chapter 5 takes a close look at the properties of dependent measures and their relationship to power. The ways in which design, sample size, and alpha can be used to amplify power are considered in Chapter 6. In Chapter 7 the role of the independent variable, that is, the treatment versus control contrast, in determining the effect size and hence statistical power comes under scrutiny. Finally, Chapter 8 summarizes all the various tactics for engendering statistical power and discusses how the researcher might integrate them in an overall strategy for treatment effectiveness research.

5. Dependent Measures

The influence of the characteristics of dependent (outcome) measures on statistical power in treatment effectiveness research deserves much broader recognition. It is, after all, those measures that yield the set of numerical values upon which statistical significance testing is performed. Each measure chosen for a study constitutes a sort of listening station for certain effects expected to result from the treatment. If the listening station is in the wrong place or is unresponsive to effects when they are present, nothing will be heard.

In particular, the characteristics of a dependent measure influence the effect size parameter in statistical power. The effect size parameter can be thought of as a signal-to-noise ratio. The signal is any difference between treatment and control group means *on the dependent measure* (the *ES* numerator, $\mu_t - \mu_c$). The noise is the within-groups variability *on that dependent measure* (the *ES* denominator, σ). Effect size and, hence, statistical power is large when the signal-to-noise ratio is high, that is, when the *ES* numerator is large relative to the *ES* denominator. It follows that the ideal measure for treatment effects is one that is maximally responsive to any changes the treatment brings about and minimally responsive to anything else.

Unfortunately, few measures have these ideal characteristics and the researcher will often have little choice but to employ measures that may not vary much in response to treatment and may vary a great deal in response to other factors. Under such circumstances the researcher needs a clear understanding of the factors that influence a measure's sensitivity so as to make the best use of what measures are available or, if necessary, to develop suitable new measures. This chapter discusses three aspects of measurement that have direct consequences for the magnitude of the effect size parameter and, therefore, statistical power: (1) validity for measuring change, (2) reliability, and (3) discrimination of individual differences among subjects.

Validity for Change

For a measure to respond to the signal, that is, to net treatment effects, it must have validity for measuring the characteristic the treatment is expected to change (Cleary, Linn, & Walster, 1970). Validity means that the measure must measure the right thing. If a treatment produces higher self-esteem, for instance, but the dependent measure is not a valid measure of self-esteem, no treatment effect will be found. But, validity alone is not sufficient to make a measure responsive to treatment effects. What is required is validity for *change*. A measure can be a valid indicator of a characteristic but still not be a valid indicator of change on that characteristic. It is known, for example, that a person's bodyweight fluctuates somewhat from day to day and during any given day. A bathroom scale, which gives a valid gross measure of weight, is generally insensitive to these small fluctuations. Validity for change means that a measure shows an observable difference when there is, in fact, a change on the characteristic measured that is of sufficient magnitude to be interesting in the context of application.

There are various ways in which a measure can lack validity for change. For one, it may be scaled in units that are too gross to detect the change. A measure of mortality (deathrate), for instance, may be quite a valid indicator of health status but insensitive to variations in how sick a person is. Graduated measures, those that range over some continuum, are generally more sensitive to change than are categorical measures, since the latter only record change between categories, not within them. The number of readmissions to a mental hospital, for example, constitutes a continuum that can differentiate one readmission from many. This continuum is often represented categorically as "readmitted" versus "not readmitted," however, with a consequent loss of sensitivity to change and statistical power (Cohen, 1983). Additionally, measurement errors can be much more serious in categorical measures than in graduated ones (Schwartz, 1985), further obscuring any real change on the characteristic of interest. It should be noted that graduated measures can, in effect, be changed to less sensitive categorical or rank-order measures by the statistical test used to analyze them. Nonparametric tests (Siegel, 1956) applied to scores on a graduated measure, for instance, generally make use of only the ordinal or categorical information in the scores with results analogous to using a coarser measurement unit to begin with. As a consequence, such tests are generally less powerful than are parametric tests (Cohen, 1982).

Another way in which a measure may lack validity for measuring change is to have a floor or ceiling that limits downward or upward response. A high school level mathematics achievement test might be quite unresponsive to improvements in Albert Einstein's understanding of mathematics—he would most likely score at the top of the scale with or without such improvements. Also, a measure may be specifically designed to cancel out certain types of change, as when scores on IQ tests are scaled by age norms to adjust away age differences in ability to answer the items correctly. In such cases, the raw scores often prove more valid for measuring change than do the age-adjusted scores.

Measures that are valid for change will respond when treatment alters the characteristic of interest and, therefore, will differentiate a treatment group from a control group. The stronger this differentiation, the greater the contrast between the group means will be and, correspondingly, the larger the effect size will be.

Reliability

Turning now to the "noise" in our signal detection analogy, we must consider variance in the dependent measure scores that may obscure any "signal" due to treatment effects. Random error variance, that is, unreliability in the measure, is obviously such a noise (Cleary & Linn, 1969; Subkoviak & Levin, 1977). Unreliability represents fluctuations in the measure that are unrelated to the characteristic being measured, including treatment effects on that characteristic. Some measurement error is intrinsic—it follows from the properties of the measure. Physical instruments, for example, may be susceptible to influences from such sources as friction, temperature, static electricity, and the like no matter how carefully they are designed and used. Self-administered tests and questionnaires, similarly, are influenced by fluctuations in respondents' attention, motivation, comprehension, and so forth.

Some measurement error is procedural; it results from inconsistent or inappropriate application of the measure rather than from its intrinsic properties. Judges or raters who must report on an observed characteristic, for instance, may not be properly trained to use the same standards for their judgment. The conditions of measurement may vary for different subjects in ways that influence their responses. Recordkeeping systems may lack quality control and be incomplete or inconsistent in what they record. The result, in all such cases, is additional variation in the distribution of scores that is unrelated to the characteristic of interest.

Also included in measurement error is systematic but irrelevant variation—response of the measure to characteristics other than the one of interest that are neither intrinsic to the measure nor results of procedural inconsistency. When these other characteristics vary differently from the one being measured, they also introduce noise into a measure. For example, frequency of arrest, which may be used to assess the effects of treatment for juvenile delinquency, indexes police behavior (e.g., patrol and arrest practices) as well as the criminal behavior of the juveniles. Similarly, self-administered mathematics tests will respond, in part, to subjects' reading skills.

Measures with higher reliability or, more generally, lower measurement error will yield less variation in the distribution of scores for subjects within experimental groups. Since within-groups variance is the basis for the denominator of the *ES* ratio, less measurement error makes that denominator smaller and the overall *ES* larger.

Discrimination of Individual Differences (Subject Heterogeneity)

Another source of systematic but often irrelevant variation that is especially important in treatment effectiveness research has to do with relatively stable individual differences on the characteristic measured. When a measure is able to discriminate strongly among subjects, the variance of its distribution of scores is increased. This variation does not represent error, since subjects may truly differ, but it nonetheless contributes to the noise variance that can obscure treatment effects. To be more concrete, consider the effects of a reading improvement program. Our primary interest in this case is in whether each individual involved shows improvement in reading level, irrespective of his or her initial reading level, reading aptitude, and so forth. The sample of students studied, however, may vary greatly on just those factors. If the measure selected is responsive to those differences, the variability may be so great as to easily overshadow any gains from treatment.

Where psychological and educational effects of treatment are at issue, an important distinction is between "psychometric" measures, designed primarily to discriminate individual differences, and "edumetric" measures, designed primarily to detect change (Carver, 1974). Psychometric measures are those developed using techniques that spread out the scores of respondents to better assess the extent to which each has a particular characteristic. IQ tests, aptitude tests, personality tests, and other such standardized tests would generally be psychometric measures.

By comparison, edumetric measures are those developed by sampling some defined content domain which represents the new responses subjects are expected to acquire as a result of treatment. Mastery tests, such as those an elementary teacher would give students to determine if they had learned to do long division, are examples of edumetric tests. Similarly, criterion referenced or domain referenced tests, in which performance on the measure is referenced to some specific level of passing performance or some specific domain of desired responses, would be classified as edumetric (Berk, 1980; Nitko, 1980; Popham, 1978).

Because they are keyed specifically to that set of responses that might be expected to result from treatment, edumetric tests or measures constructed along similar lines in noneducational areas are more sensitive to the changes induced by treatment and less sensitive to preexisting individual differences. To the extent that any measure reflects less heterogeneity among subjects, within-group variability on that measure is smaller. That, in turn, results in a smaller denominator for the *ES* ratio and a corresponding increase in statistical power.

A Framework for Analyzing Candidate Dependent Measures

The importance of having valid, reliable, and sensitive dependent measures in treatment effectiveness research is so great that it will generally warrant considerable advance preparation. An appropriate sequence might be as follows: First, any relevant theory, experience, previous information, and common sense pertinent to treatment effects should be used to identify and define systematically the change expected to result from treatment that is of sufficient interest to be measured. Then, candidate measures for those effects should be identified or, if necessary, created. Following this, investigation should be made of whether those measures have sufficient validity, reliability, and sensitivity to detect any change of interest under the research design planned. Final selection of the dependent measures to be used in the research should be based on the results of that investigation.

What we want to look at now is how one might investigate the properties of various candidate measures. Three phases of such an investigation can be identified. One is to examine the intrinsic nature of the measure or the basis for its construction and determine whether, on logical and conceptual grounds, it is an appropriate measure. The second step is to review previous research using the measure in order to determine whether it has demonstrated the necessary properties empirically. Finally, it will often be necessary to conduct a measurement assessment study to investigate the properties of the measure, diagnose any problems, and provide guidance for appropriate modification. Because a measurement assessment study is the most probing type of investigation, we will focus on it in this chapter. The issues that arise in that context are the same as those that would be considered when examining the intrinsic nature of a measure or its research literature; only the form is different.

Measurement Assessment Study

A measurement assessment study tries out candidate dependent measures on appropriate subjects prior to implementation of any treatment in such a way that useful information about the properties of the measures is obtained. The results of such a study may simply confirm that a measure is adequate for treatment effectiveness research. More likely, however, it will identify some adjustments or alterations that will improve measurement.

The points upon which we want to assess candidate dependent measures are those identified above as most relevant to statistical power: validity for change, reliability, and response to subject heterogeneity. Since the latter two issues both have to do with the variability on the measure, they must be considered together.

Validity for change. In the physical sciences, the sensitivity and accuracy of a measurement instrument are often checked by applying it to samples of known characteristics to determine if the correct results are produced. An analogous approach can be taken in the social sciences using a criterion group contrast of the sort described in Chapter 3. A criterion group contrast, recall, is a comparison between two groups known to differ on the characteristic that treatment is expected to change. Such a contrast must be defined in a way that ensures that the difference represented is of sufficient magnitude to have importance in the context of interest, but is in the range of what can reasonably be expected as a treatment versus control group difference. Various candidate measures are then applied to the criterion contrast, and effect sizes are constructed to indicate how well each discriminates between the criterion groups. A measure that is sensitive to the criterion contrast should also be sensitive to differences of similar magnitude between the treatment and control group and, therefore, be a valid measure of the change that produces those differences.

In addition to representing a difference judged to be meaningful and in the range of what effective treatment might produce, there are some other desirable characteristics of criterion group contrasts. In particular, the subject samples involved should be as much like those to be used in the planned treatment effectiveness research as possible. The samples should be similar in their mean values on the measures of interest so that any floor or ceiling effects will be disclosed. They should also be similar in their variability on the candidate measures so that the resulting effect sizes will be representative of what might occur under treatment. Additionally, of course, the samples should be large enough to yield stable estimates of the criterion group differences on each measure of interest.

It may be possible to locate appropriate criterion group contrast on the measures of interest in the published research literature. The most informative situation is to find experimental studies in which the treatments, samples, and measures are similar to those planned. *If* those studies show large effects, it indicates that the measures at issue must have validity for measuring change. The results are equivocal if the effects are not large, however—either ineffective treatment or unresponsive measures might yield that outcome. Another approach, therefore, is to look for research in which the dependent measures of interest were used to compare large subject groups with prior differences rather than experimental groups. For example, if the planned treatment effectiveness research involves elementary school subjects and achievement test measures, the researcher might look for research in which students at different grade levels were compared on the candidate tests. If those tests can strongly discriminate the abilities of, say, third graders in comparison to fourth graders, then they should be valid measures for treatment effects of that same order of magnitude.

In many situations, however, the research literature will not yield sufficient information about the validity for change of a measure of interest, and the researcher will want to study the matter directly. Two rather different examples will illustrate how a criterion group contrast study can be constructed to evaluate candidate dependent measures. Consider first the example presented in Chapter 3 on recidivism measures to assess the effects of juvenile delinquency treatment programs. In that example a criterion group contrast was developed between juveniles judged by police to be minor offenders and those judged to be more serious offenders. In Chapter 3, interest focused on how a researcher might determine the *ES* expected in a treatment effectiveness study or, alternatively, assess the practical significance of one already obtained.

This same example, however, can be examined with regard to what the criterion contrast can tell us about the sensitivity of various candidate recidivism measures. Recidivism measures based on police records can be defined in many ways—rearrested versus not rearrested, number of rearrests, severity of offenses for which rearrested, time to first rearrest, and

TABLE 5.1 Effect Sizes on Various Six-Month Recidivism Measures for a Contrast Between Minor and More Serious Delinquents (N = 1630)

Measure	Effect size (ES) for contrast
Rearrested/not rearrested dichotomy	.32
Number of rearrests (frequency)	.26
Average rearrest severity	.32
Lag time to first rearrest	.33
Frequency, severity, lag composite	.33

SOURCE: Lipsey, 1982

so forth. A measurement assessment study might be used to determine whether some versions of this measure are more sensitive to a given contrast than others. Table 5.1 shows the result, in *ES* terms, of comparing the sample of minor offenders with the sample of more serious offenders on various recidivism measures.

Table 5.1 tells the researcher that there is relatively little difference among the various recidivism measures in their sensitivity to this criterion group contrast. The composite measure and the lag time measure show the largest response by a small margin, and the frequency measure shows the smallest response. The simple dichotomy, rearrested versus not rearrested, does about as well as any of the more detailed measures, despite its crudeness. More importantly, this analysis shows that even the best of these measures is not very valid for measurement of change in treatment effectiveness research. The difference in amount of delinquency between the two criterion groups is larger than that which treatment is likely to produce, yet it only represented effect sizes in the range of .26 to .33. Given that the researcher wished to be able to detect treatment effects smaller than this contrast, the demands on statistical power are considerable. The researcher must therefore either plan a study with large samples or find a more sensitive dependent measure.

A second example comes from Schery's (1981) study of children with language disorders in special education classes. A considerable variety of standardized language measures have been used with such students. It was uncertain, however, which if any of the available measures would be sensitive to any gains these students made during treatment. A criterion group contrast for this situation was constructed from school records reporting the results of a large testing battery administered annually to the children

TABLE 5.2 Effect Sizes on Various Language Measures for a Three-Year
Pre-Post Contrast on Special Education Students (*N* = 700)

Measure	Effect size (ES) for contrast
Peabody (raw scores)	.81
Peabody (scaled scores)	.20
ITPA Auditory Reception	.77
ITPA Auditory Association	.94
ITPA Verbal Expression	1.06
ITPA Grammatical Closure	.87
ITPA Auditory Memory	.63
NSST Receptivity	.87
NSST Expressivity	.81
Elicited imitation	.74
WISC Verbal	.00

NOTE: ITPA = Illinois Test of Psycholinguistic Ability; NSST = Northwestern Syntax Screening Test;
WISC = Wechsler Intelligence Scale for Children.
SOURCE: Lipsey, 1983

in the programs. The criterion contrast was defined by comparing children with complete test batteries at the time of enrollment in special education classes with the same children approximately three years later. The rationale for this comparison as a basis for assessing the measures' validity for change was that three years of combined maturation and training made a difference in the language ability of the children that was clearly observable by teachers and parents and thus should be measurable. Note that the interest at this point is in assessing the sensitivity of various candidate dependent measures, not in assessing the effects of treatment which, of course, are confounded with natural developmental change in this criterion contrast.

Table 5.2 displays the response of various language measures to the criterion contrast as defined above. There were substantial differences among the measures. The WISC Verbal IQ measure, for example, showed virtually no response to the criterion contrast, as might be expected given that IQ is generally defined as a stable individual characteristic not subject to change. The Peabody Picture Vocabulary Test, a widely used language measure, was relatively insensitive to the criterion contrast when the scores were age scaled, but showed good contrast when raw scores were used. The researcher, therefore, discovers a very simple way to make this test more valid for measuring change.

Another interesting facet of the comparisons in Table 5.2 is the differ-

ential response of the various subscales of the Illinois Test of Psycholinguistic Ability (ITPA). Some of these scales (e.g., Verbal Expression)
showed greater contrast between the criterion groups than others (e.g., Au-
ditory Memory). Since the scales are designed to measure somewhat different aspects of language ability, however, a confounding arises that is
characteristic of this situation of comparing different measures for a given
criterion contrast. Differential response can result because measures of the
same characteristic have different sensitivity to change or because they
measure different characteristics, some of which have not changed as much
as others in the chosen criterion contrast. Since the researcher must determine both what characteristics respond to treatment and how to measure
those changes, the information from a carefully chosen criterion group
contrast is still useful to the planned treatment effectiveness study despite
its ambiguity on this point.

As these examples illustrate, comparing the effect sizes resulting from a
criterion group contrast yields information about the overall response of
various measures to group differences analogous to those that might result
from treatment effects. Further assessment of candidate dependent measures requires a closer examination of the variance of each over the population of interest. We turn now to that topic.

Reliability and subject heterogeneity. When comparing two populations or samples from those populations, the larger the variance on the
scores within each grouping, the smaller the effect size will be since that
variance is the basis for the denominator of the *ES* ratio. A recurring theme
of this volume is that the effect size in any treatment effectiveness study
would be enhanced, with beneficial effects on power, if the amount of
within-groups variance, the noise in the *ES* signal-noise ratio, could be
reduced. As pointed out earlier, one source of such variance is the unreliability of the measure (or, more generally, the measurement error)—variability in scores unrelated to the characteristic being measured. Another
source is the heterogeneity of subjects on the measure, that is, the extent to
which the measure differentiates subjects.

Note that these two variance sources represent, respectively, variance
related to the characteristic being measured (subject heterogeneity) and
variance unrelated to that characteristic (measurement error). Defined this
way, these two sources necessarily account for the total variance within a
distribution of scores since all variance must be either related or unrelated
to the true values. More specifically, we are adopting the formulation
of classic measurement theory (see also Guilford, 1954) which divides

each observed score X for subject i into a true component and an error component: that is, $X_i = T_i + e_i$. When the error component is uncorrelated with the true score component and randomly distributed, the variance of the true values and that of the error sum to the total variance: that is $\sigma_x^2 = \sigma_T^2 + \sigma_e^2$.

Each of these two different variance components requires different tactics if it is to be reduced so as to enhance the operative *ES* in a treatment effectiveness study. What is needed from a measurement assessment study, therefore, is a diagnosis of the relative contribution of measurement error and subject heterogeneity to the total within-groups variance so the researcher will know which constitutes the greatest problem. We will first examine some ways to differentiate measurement error from subject heterogeneity, then discuss ways the researcher might reduce each.

The simplest approach to analyzing within-groups variability is to estimate the reliability of a measure directly in variance terms. The reliability coefficient indexes the amount of measurement error in the scores and, since there are only two categories of variance at issue, subject heterogeneity can be estimated by subtracting the measurement error variance from the total variance. The reliability of a measure can be expressed in variance terms as follows (Winer, 1971):

$$\rho_x = \frac{\sigma_T^2}{\sigma_T^2 + \sigma_e^2} \qquad \text{[A]}$$

Where ρ_x is the reliability parameter for the population, σ_T^2 is the variance among subjects in the true score component of the measure X, and σ_E^2 is the variance in the error component.

In other words, the reliability of a measure is simply the proportion of the total variance (defined as $\sigma_T^2 + \sigma_e^2$) that is due to the true difference among subjects. It follows that if we have an estimate of the variance on a measure of interest (σ_x^2) and a reliability coefficient that estimates its reliability (ρ_x), we can divide the variance into two components: the subject heterogeneity component, estimated as $\rho\sigma^2$, and the measurement error component, estimated as $(1 - \rho)\sigma^2$. Since effect size is defined as $(\mu_t - \mu_c)/\sigma$, it can be expressed in turn as:

$$ES = \frac{\mu_t - \mu_c}{\sqrt{\rho_x\sigma_x^2 + (1 - \rho_x)\sigma_x^2}} \qquad \text{[B]}$$

Given an estimate of the reliability of a measure, therefore, and an estimate of the total variance on that measure for a sample of subjects of interest, the researcher can partition the *ES* denominator into the subject heterogeneity component and the measurement error component. It is then relatively easy to determine which component contributes the most variability to the *ES* denominator and the extent to which *ES* would increase if either error or subject heterogeneity (or both) were reduced by a given amount. For example, by setting $(1 - \rho_x)\sigma_x^2 = 0$ in equation [B] above, we can estimate the increase in *ES* that would result if the dependent measure were made perfectly reliable $(\rho_x = 1.00)$. Or, by multiplying $\rho_x\sigma_x^2$ by .5, we can estimate the increase in *ES* that would result if the subject heterogeneity variance on that measure could be halved, and so forth.

A broader framework within which to consider the sources of variance in a measure of interest is the random effects analysis of variance model, more specifically, a components of variance model (Cronbach, Gleser, Nanda, & Rajaratnam, 1972; Lipsey, 1983). This approach has the advantage of permitting a more probing examination of the sources of variability represented in a candidate measure. In this framework the researcher conducts a measurement assessment study by setting up an analysis of variance design that includes as a factor each aspect of a measure that may be a source of important variability. For example, to examine classic reliability (variation from occasion to occasion) and subject heterogeneity, a design would be constructed in which multiple subjects were each measured on multiple occasions, as shown in the schematic of Table 5.3.

The design shown in Table 5.3 allows us to partition the total variance obtained on the measure (σ_x^2) into three components—variation among subjects (σ_s^2); variation among occasions (σ_o^2); and residual error (σ_e^2), which is everything left over. The way this is done is to compute the mean square values (*MS*) from the data in the typical fashion, as described in basic ANOVA texts (see Kirk, 1982) or performed by appropriate computer programs (e.g., SPSS, BMDP). Usually those mean square values would be turned into F-ratios and used to test statistical significance. Our purpose here, however, is to use them to partition the total variance into its components. To do this we recognize that each mean square estimates the value of some linear combination of some of the variance components in which we are interested. These linear combinations are called the expected mean squares (*EMS*) and their formulations, which differ for each ANOVA design, are generally given in ANOVA texts (Kirk, 1982, is especially good in this regard).

By setting up the *EMS* formulations as simultaneous equations and solv-

TABLE 5.3 Design Schematic for a Random Effects Components of Variance Analysis to Partition Subject Heterogeneity Variance from Residual Measurement Error Variance

		Occasions					
		01	*02*	.	.	.	*0j*
Subjects	S1	x_{11}	x_{12}	–	–	–	x_{1j}
	S2	x_{21}	x_{22}	–	–	–	x_{2j}
	S3	x_{31}	x_{32}	–	–	–	x_{3j}
	S4	x_{41}	x_{42}	–	–	–	x_{4j}
	.	–	–	–	–	–	–
	.	–	–	–	–	–	–
	.						
	Sn	x_{n1}	x_{n2}	–	–	–	x_{nj}

NOTE: x_{nj} is the score on the measure of interest for the *n*th subject on the *j*th occasion.

	ANOVA summary		
Source	*df*	*MS*	*EMS*
Between occasions (O)	$j-1$	MS_O	$\sigma_e^2 + n\sigma_o^2$
Between subjects (S)	$n-1$	MS_S	$\sigma_e^2 + j\sigma_s^2$
Residual error	$(j-1)(n-1)$	MS_E	σ_e^2

NOTE: n = number of subjects; j = number of occasions.

ing them for the individual variance components, an estimate of each component can be made. For example, from the ANOVA summary in Table 5.3 we have the following as simultaneous equations where σ_e^2 represents the residual error term, σ_o^2 represents the variance among j occasions of measurement, and σ_s^2 represents the variance among n subjects:

$$MS_o = \sigma_e^2 + \sigma_o^2$$
$$MS_s = \sigma_e^2 + j\sigma_s^2$$
$$MS_E = \sigma_e^2$$

If actual data were to produce values of $MS_O = 2.5$ for $j = 2$, $MS_S = 22.2$ for $n = 20$, and $MS_E = 2.4$ then we would have equations as follows:

$$2.5 = \sigma_e^2 + 20\sigma_o^2$$
$$22.2 = \sigma_e^2 + 2\sigma_s^2$$
$$2.4 = \sigma_e^2$$

With some simple algebra, we obtain the following estimates for each variance component:

$$\sigma_s^2 = 9.9 \quad \sigma_o^2 = 0.0 \quad \sigma_e^2 = 2.4 \text{ and } \sigma_x^2 = \sigma_o^2 + \sigma_s^2 + \sigma_e^2 = 12.3$$

We need now to interpret these variance components in ways that help us better understand the properties of the measure we are investigating. The term σ_s^2 represents the variation among subject scores averaged over occasions. It is thus a direct indicator of subject heterogeneity—variation among subjects in that portion of their scores that does not fluctuate from occasion to occasion. The term σ_e^2 represents residual error—in particular, the variability in scores that is not accounted for either by mean differences among subjects nor mean differences among occasions. It thus indicates the measurement error—the random component of these scores that fluctuates from occasion to occasion for each subject.

The remaining term, σ_o^2, represents the variation among occasions averaged over subjects, that is, whether the mean value for this group of subjects is different from one occasion to the next. This component would pick up any trends or fluctuations over time for the whole group. Variance from this source would not affect the distribution of within-group scores in an actual treatment effectiveness study if all subjects were measured at the same time, as is usually done. Moreover, in the test-retest reliability situation represented here, there should be little change in the group mean so long as the interval between testings is short, and this component will therefore be virtually zero. More generally, when doing a measurement assessment study using the components of variance approach, we can simply discard any variance component that would not appear in the actual treatment effectiveness study planned and thus be irrelevant to the total within-groups variance of that study. Alternatively, such components can be forced to zero by standardizing the data separately for each column or row of data across which the irrelevant variation in the means occurs. For example, separately standardizing each column of data in Table 5.3, that is, subtracting the column mean from each score and dividing the result by the column standard deviation, will force σ_o^2 to zero by giving each column a zero mean with no variation among them.

For the present example, therefore, the total variance from Table 5.3 relevant to effect size can be represented as the sum of the subject heterogeneity component σ_s^2 and the residual error component σ_e^2. Moreover, we see that of a total variance of 12.3 in the numerical example, 80% of it is subject heterogeneity (9.9/12.3) and 20% of it is residual measurement error (2.4/12.3). Using formula [A] presented earlier for reliability, and recognizing that σ_s^2 corresponds to σ_T^2, we find that the proportion of total variance represented by subject heterogeneity (e.g., .80 in this case) estimates the reliability coefficient directly.

Our primary interest, however, is the formulation of the effect size parameter *ES*. The components of variance analysis has separated the within-groups variance term that is the denominator of the *ES* ratio into two components, one representing subject heterogeneity and one representing measurement error. We can therefore represent *ES* as follows:

$$ES = \frac{\mu_t - \mu_c}{\sqrt{\sigma_s^2 + \sigma_e^2}} \qquad [C]$$

The utility of this formulation, as with the analogous equation [B] earlier, is that it allows us to examine directly the role in *ES* of the responsiveness of our candidate dependent measure to individual differences among subjects (σ_s^2) and of its measurement error (σ_e^2). In particular, it allows us to identify sources of within-group variation that deflate *ES* and, correspondingly, statistical power. Such a diagnosis points the way to alterations in the design or measurement plan that may reduce that variance and make the research more sensitive to treatment effects.

The example of components of variance analysis presented in Table 5.3 examines measurement error only in terms of the stability or reliability over multiple occasions of measurement. The advantage of the components of variance approach relative to working directly with a reliability coefficient as in equation [B] is that the former can be easily adapted to study other sources of measurement error beside instability over time. Suppose, for example, that a researcher was concerned about measurement error stemming from differences among raters in a situation where the dependent measure of interest was clinicians' ratings of the progress of their patients. In this situation, a measurement assessment study could be conducted in which variation over raters instead of occasions was examined. The study format would be as in Table 5.3, but each column in the data matrix would represent a different rater's scores for each subject in the sample. Interpretation of the resulting variance components would, as before, distinguish subject heterogeneity from measurement error. In this case, however, the measurement error component would inform us of problems with inconsistency among raters rather than instability over occasions.

Similarly, components of variance analysis in a measurement assessment study might be used to examine error variance stemming from use of different measurement instruments (e.g., scales, meters, test forms), procedural differences in administering measures, different settings, and the like. More complex measurement studies can also be conducted in which several measurement facets are varied within the same design. When that is done, the measurement error variance component, σ_e^2, can be further decomposed into the portions stemming from each of the facets represented, plus a residual error not otherwise accounted for. Detailed description of these more differentiated measurement assessment studies is beyond the scope of the present volume but can be found in Cronbach et al. (1972) and Brennan (1980) under the label of "generalizability theory." Specific examples of application can be found in Green, Nguyen, and Attkisson (1979), Lipsey (1983), and Mazzeo and Seeley (1984).

For present purposes, another look at the delinquency and language disorders examples presented earlier will illustrate how the components of variance approach can be used to identify sources of within-group variance that may degrade statistical power. The second of those examples, recall, involved a battery of language measures administered over a three-year interval to a sample of language handicapped children. If we look at these data simply as candidate dependent measures administered on two occasions of measurement, we have exactly the design depicted in Table 5.3. The criterion group contrast of interest earlier is analogous to σ_0^2 in that design but, since it is not relevant to the within-groups variability, we will set it equal to zero in this instance.

The relative size of the two variance components of interest for each measure is shown in Table 5.4. Note that for every measure the subject heterogeneity component, σ_s^2, is larger, often much larger, than the residual error component σ_e^2. Since the variance components in Table 5.4 are each presented as a proportion of the total within-groups variance, that is, as a proportion of $\sigma_s^2 + \sigma_e^2$, the figures in the σ_s^2 column can be read directly as reliability coefficients ($\sigma_s^2/(\sigma_s^2 + \sigma_e^2)$ as in equation [A]). For most of the measures, the reliability is in the range of .70 to .99. Considering that these data essentially represent test-retest reliability over a three-year interval rather than the usual interval of a few weeks, the reliability of these mea-

TABLE 5.4 Relative Size of the Subject Heterogeneity and Residual Error Variance Components of Various Language Measures on Special Education Students (*N* = 700)

	Proportion of within-groups variance	
Measure	σ_s^2	σ_e^2
Peabody (raw scores)	.85	.15
Peabody (scaled scores)	.56	.44
ITPA Auditory Reception	.78	.22
ITPA Auditory Association	.85	.15
ITPA Verbal Expression	.72	.28
ITPA Grammatical Closure	.82	.18
ITPA Auditory Memory	.88	.12
NSST Receptivity	.75	.25
NSST Expressivity	.81	.19
Elicited imitation	.85	.15
WISC Verbal	.99	.01

NOTE: ITPA = Illinois Test of Psycholinguistic Ability; NSST = Northwestern Syntax Screening Test; WISC = Wechsler Intelligence Scale for Children.
SOURCE: Lipsey, 1983

sures is clearly quite good. This result is typical of standardized psychometric measures—they are strong indicators of individual differences and characteristically have high reliability.

Treatment effectiveness research using these language measures, therefore, would be made considerably more powerful if the subject heterogeneity variance component could be reduced. By comparison, improving the reliability would make little difference since it is already quite good (that is, σ_e^2 is relatively small). For instance, Table 5.4 shows that the subject heterogeneity variance component constitutes 85% of the within-groups variance on the raw scores from the Peabody Picture Vocabulary Test. If a way could be found to reduce that component by half, that is, to .42 variance units, it would decrease the *ES* denominator from 1.00 to .75 variance units (i.e., from $\sqrt{.85 + .15}$ to $\sqrt{.42 + .15}$). The operative *ES*, correspondingly, would increase by one-third (i.e., from $(\mu_t - \mu_c)/1.00\sigma$ to $(\mu_t - \mu_c)/.75\sigma = 1.33(\mu_t - \mu_c)/\sigma)$.

The recidivism measures for juvenile delinquency presented earlier in Table 5.1 provide a contrasting example. Table 5.5 displays the results of a components of variance analysis for them. These components were derived from an ANOVA in which two occasions of measurement were compared, the arrest record for six months prior to the disposition that defined

TABLE 5.5 Relative Size of the Subject Heterogeneity and Residual Error Variance Components for Various Recidivism Measures on Delinquents (N = 1630)

Measure	Proportion of within-groups variance σ_s^2	σ_e^2
Rearrested/not rearrested dichotomy	.21	.79
Number of rearrests (frequency)	.24	.76
Average rearrest severity	.21	.79
Lag time to first rearrest	.22	.78
Frequency, severity, lag composite	.26	.74

SOURCE: Lipsey, 1982

the criterion group membership and that for six months afterwards. That is, this was another simple test-retest reliability design like that shown in Table 5.3.

It is clear in Table 5.5 that the problem with these delinquency measures is not subject heterogeneity, as with the language measures, but high measurement error. The residual error variance component ranges from .74 for the composite measure to .79 for the dichotomous and severity measures. Since these are proportions of total within-group variance ($\sigma_s^2 + \sigma_e^2$), the corresponding reliability coefficients ($1 - \sigma_e^2$) are in the range of .21 to .26 which, of course, represent extremely low values.

This information gives us a better understanding of why the effect sizes for the criterion group contrast examined earlier were so small (Table 5.1). With approximately 75% of their variance reflecting only measurement error, any response of these measures to group differences would be heavily masked by this random noise component. A researcher planning to use one of these measures in a treatment effectiveness study could not expect a very large ES nor, correspondingly, much statistical power with modest sample size unless some way were found to improve their reliability substantially.

The amount by which the operative ES using one of these delinquency measures can be increased by reducing the size of the σ_e^2 variance component can be estimated in the same general fashion as for the previous example using language measures. We know from Table 5.5 that each unit of within-groups variance for, say, the rearrested/not rearrested dichotomy is 79% measurement error; that is, the reliability coefficient is .21 (or $1 - .79$). If we could increase the reliability of this measure to .80, it would mean that only 20% of the variance could be measurement error.

That would correspond to a reduction in σ_e^2 from .79 to .05 variance units (making the total variance, .21 + .05, equal to about .26 variance units of which 20% or .05/.26 is measurement error). The *ES* denominator would thus decrease from 1.00 standard deviation unit to .51 (i.e., $\sqrt{.26}$). The overall *ES*, correspondingly, would increase by a factor of 1/.51 = 1.96. The result of substantially improving the reliability of this measure, therefore, is to almost double the operative *ES*. The criterion group contrast estimates in Table 5.1, for instance, would increase from around *ES* = .30 to about *ES* = .60. This is a large increment that would yield a dramatic improvement in power.

How Can Subject Heterogeneity and Measurement Error Be Reduced?

The importance of examining the components of variance for a dependent measure of interest for treatment effectiveness research, as suggested above, is to diagnose and control those sources of variability that diminish the *ES* parameter and, hence, statistical power. How, then, does a researcher manage to reduce subject heterogeneity or measurement error on a measure? A detailed discussion is beyond the scope of this book and, in any event, is available in most experimental design or measurement textbooks (see Myers, 1979, chap. 6; Stanley, 1971). It may be useful, however, to review the general strategies that a treatment effectiveness researcher may be able to use.

Subject heterogeneity. There are two broad strategies available for minimizing the amount of subject heterogeneity represented in the within-groups variance on a dependent measure. First, measures can be selected or developed which do not discriminate strongly among subjects. Second, if the measure does respond substantially to subject differences, an attempt can be made during data analysis to remove that component statistically from the variance.

The nature of measures that respond minimally to individual differences among subjects on a given characteristic while still responding to change on that characteristic was mentioned earlier in the discussion on mastery, criterion-referenced, or edumetric measures (Carver, 1974). Measures of this sort are particularly useful for assessing the effects of treatments that are expected to result in new responses that were not present or possible prior to treatment—new behaviors, new knowledge, new attitudes, and the like. In these cases, measures can often be developed which are directed specifically to that new response domain. Since those responses are unlikely to occur for any subject prior to treatment, little differences among subjects show up on such measures at that point. The emergence of the new responses after treatment, however, produces distinct pre-post changes on the measure for treated subjects and a corresponding contrast on mean scores for treatment and control subjects.

The best known examples of such measures come from education, where instructional "treatment" is generally expected to result in new knowledge or skills. A mastery test given by a teacher in a classroom to determine if the students have learned the material covered in the lessons is an edumetric measure. If the lessons, for instance, cover adding and subtracting fractions, most students will score rather poorly prior to instruction on a test dealing exclusively with that topic and much better afterward. Indeed, it is possible that all students would score zero without instruction and 100% with it. A carefully constructed mastery test, therefore, can virtually eliminate individual differences in scores while responding strongly to change. Discussions of such tests and their variants in education are found in the literature on mastery testing, criterion-referenced testing, domain-referenced testing, instructional sensitivity, and the like (see Berk, 1980; Haladyna & Roid, 1981; Hanna & Bennett, 1984; Nitko, 1980; Popham, 1978).

While used most extensively in education, the "mastery" testing approach can also be used in other areas where treatment is expected to produce something new. What is required is first to define the domain of new behaviors, characteristics, or whatever that are expected to appear. Then a measure is constructed that is keyed as much as possible to that domain, that is, responds when one of the new characteristics is present and does not respond otherwise. Physical therapy for stroke patients, for example, might be assessed by identifying the functions most commonly lost after a stroke—like control of certain muscles—then measuring ability on specifically those functions.

In situations where the effects of treatment are to strengthen or weaken existing characteristics rather than create new ones, on the other hand, it will generally be difficult or impossible to create measures that are both responsive to change and unresponsive to individual differences among subjects. In these circumstances, the best strategy is to try to reduce statistically the subject heterogeneity variance in the scores during data analysis. This is accomplished by first building into the study design some other variable that is strongly correlated with the dependent measure, that is, a variable that strongly covaries with the individual differences across subjects. Any variance among the scores that is systematically associated with such a covariate can then be statistically removed, virtually subtracted out, with the result that within-groups variance is reduced by that amount.

The procedures for accomplishing this sort of variance reduction in experimental design and analysis include repeated measures or paired subjects designs, blocked or stratified designs, analysis of covariance, and hierarchical multiple regression. In Chapter 4, many of these procedures were listed as "statistical tests," and their influence on the variance term in the *ES* denominator was formulated for purposes of estimating statistical power from the power charts in that chapter. Chapter 6, which follows this one, also discusses this issue. Since this technique is more closely related to matters of design and analysis than to measurement, no further discussion is presented here.

Measurement error. The strategies available to researchers for improving the reliability of measurement also fall into two broad categories: 1) some form of procedural or experimental control can be used to prevent or minimize measurement error, or 2) some form of aggregation or averaging of multiple individually errorful measures can be used to reduce the influence of error on the composite scores.

"Procedural or administrative control" refers to those steps the researcher can take before and during the measurement process to minimize the possibility that scores will reflect anything but the characteristic being measured. At the outset, measures can be selected or developed to have high inherent reliability—for example, through item-analysis procedures (Gulliksen, 1950). Additionally, every effort can be made to maintain consistency in all aspects of the application of a measure to which it may be responsive. Reliability may be improved, for instance, when instructions for self-administered tests are presented in consistent fashion to all subjects, when measurement is always conducted in the same setting, and so forth. For other sorts of measures, there are analogous procedural issues—for example, having identical training regimens for raters, using the same meter to take all readings, and the like. These matters can be very specific to particular measurement instruments and circumstances; therefore, careful analysis of the exact context of application is required to determine which aspects of the measurement procedures are most important to keep constant. The general principle here, however, is for the researcher to identify every feature of the circumstances of measurement that may influence the resulting scores, then keep each such feature as constant as possible during measurement so that minimal error is introduced.

Improving reliability by using multiple measures and aggregating their individual values into a composite measure takes advantage of the fact that the error component of a measure is, by its very nature, inconsistent. If, for example, two measured values are added together, and the error components of their respective scores are uncorrelated, those error portions will combine in a haphazard way—sometimes creating a positive sum larger than either component, sometimes a negative sum, and other times canceling each other out. The components of the scores representing any characteristic the two measures both respond to in common, however, should always be in the same direction and thus sum to larger values than either component. The net result, as more and more such measures are combined, is that the "true score" component of the resulting composite become larger relative to the error component. This is the logic of multi-item tests or scales—each individual item may have only a modest true score component, but when a sufficient number are combined, the composite can be quite reliable. Similarly, the ratings of individual judges can be aggregated into a composite more reliable than the rating of any single judge, results from different test forms can be aggregated, readings from different meters can be averaged, observations from different occasions can be combined, and so forth (Cascio, Valenzi, & Silbey, 1980; Epstein, 1980; Green et al., 1979; Levin & Subkoviak, 1977, 1978; Stanley, 1971).

Conclusions

This chapter argues that certain properties of the dependent measure in treatment effectiveness research have a large influence on statistical power because of their role in the effect size parameter. If a researcher is to have a high probability of detecting effects, the dependent measures chosen for the research must be sensitive to those effects. Measurement sensitivity in this context means that measured values fully reflect any change of interest on the characteristic measured and do not reflect an appreciable amount of noise, that is, variance from any other source.

These two considerations correspond respectively to the numerator and the denominator of the *ES* parameter. A muted response of a measure to treatment group change, that is, low validity for measuring change, restricts the difference between the treatment group and control group means and reduces *ES* by making its numerator smaller. Similarly, a large amount of heterogeneity among subjects or measurement error in the scores a measure yields will make *ES* smaller by enlarging the within-group variance upon which the *ES* denominator is based.

The message of this chapter is that a researcher who wishes to design treatment effectiveness research that has high statistical power must pay close attention to the nature of the dependent measures that will be used. If the properties of those measures are not already well-documented in the research literature, it is advisable to investigate them by conducting one or more measurement assessment studies. The results will help a researcher diagnose the shortcomings of candidate dependent measures and, if necessary, take steps to improve their sensitivity to treatment effects.

6. Design, Sample Size, and Alpha

This chapter will focus on the relationship between statistical power and selected aspects of what is conventionally called research design. By research design is meant those features of the research that must be specified by the researcher in the planning phase—what subject comparisons will be made, the sample size, the statistical test for significance testing, and so forth. Excluded are issues involving the specific nature of the dependent variables, which were discussed in the last chapter, and issues involving the specific nature of the independent variable, discussed in the next chapter.

We will first turn attention to the effect size parameter, in particular, the variance term in the *ES* denominator. As discussed in Chapter 5, one component of that variance represents subject heterogeneity, that is, the individual differences among subjects on a dependent measure. One way to reduce the influence of subject heterogeneity is with research designs that allow some statistical control of variance when the treatment versus control group difference is tested for statistical significance. As was described in Chapter 4, the *ES* formulations for many statistical tests involve adjustments to the variance term in the denominator that increase statistical power. At this point we will take a closer look at the research designs that make such adjustments possible.

Significance Testing and Error Variance

In the general case of testing the statistical significance of a treatment effect, the difference between the treatment and control group means $(\bar{X}_t - \bar{X}_c)$ is compared to an estimate of the standard error of the difference between means (*se*) to determine if the ratio is larger than some critical value. A t-test comparison, for example, would construct the ratio $(\bar{X}_t - \bar{X}_c)/se$ and compare it to the value of *t* corresponding to the available degrees of freedom and the selected alpha level.

The standard error of the difference between means depends upon two factors—the sample size and the variability of values in the population from which the sample is drawn. If there is no variability in the population—that is, all the values are the same—every sample drawn from it will have the same mean and the standard error will be zero. Thus the standard error is, in part, an index of variability within the population. Not surprisingly, it is estimated from variability within the sample. Putting sample size aside for the moment, significance testing can be thought of as a comparison of how large the difference between the group means is relative to the variability within the groups. It is because of this, of course, that *ES* (which is exactly that ratio) is an important determinant of statistical power.

But what if all of the within-groups variability is somehow not an appropriate basis for judging the magnitude of a treatment effect? We saw in Chapter 5 that the variability of scores on a dependent measure can represent large individual differences among subjects as well as measurement error. Some portion of that subject heterogeneity may derive from factors that are irrelevant to the treatment issues under investigation—so-called "nuisance" variables that can obscure the relationship of interest.

Recycling an example from Chapter 4 will help illustrate the point. A sports psychologist is interested in the effects of mental rehearsal on the times it takes athletes to run a 400-meter race. A large portion of the variability in times among runners, however, is due to the difference between males and females. The researcher does not think that an effect of mental rehearsal must be large relative to the gender differences in order to be meaningful. It may be judged sufficient if the effect for males is large relative to the variability of males and the effect for females is large relative to the variability of females. What is desired, therefore, is to somehow remove the variance associated with gender from the "error" term used to test statistical significance. Within the statistical power framework, this would correspond to removing the variance associated with gender from the *ES* denominator, resulting, of course, in a larger overall *ES* and greater power.

There are various experimental design formats and associated analysis procedures for accomplishing some adjustment of the error variance in significance testing if information is available for each subject on the nuisance variable at issue. What is important for present purposes is to recognize that when any of these designs is used, corresponding adjustments are made in the *ES* denominator for statistical power analysis. Stated generally, the denominator of *ES* should be the common (or pooled) standard deviation of the distributions of population values whose variances are the basis

TABLE 6.1 Design Format for a Treatment Versus Control Comparison with Gender as a Blocking Factor

| | | Groups ($k = 2$) | |
		Treatment	Control
Blocks			
($j = 2$)		x_{111}	x_{121}
	Male	x_{112}	x_{122}
		x_{113}	x_{123}
		—	—
		—	—
		x_{11n}	x_{12n}
		x_{211}	x_{221}
	Female	x_{212}	x_{222}
		x_{213}	x_{223}
		—	—
		—	—
		x_{21n}	x_{22n}

x_{jkn} is the score for subject n in treatment k and block j.

| | ANOVA summary | | | |
Source	Associated variance component	df	MS	F
Groups (G)	σ_G^2	$k-1$	MS_G	MS_G/MS_E
Blocks (B)	σ_B^2	$j-1$	MS_B	MS_B/MS_E
G x B	σ_{GB}^2	$(k-1)(j-1)$	MS_{GB}	MS_{GB}/MS_E
W/in cell (E)	σ_E^2	$kj(n-1)$	MS_E	

for estimating the standard error, or error term, upon which significance testing is based.

The necessary adjustments to *ES* for the most common designs and corresponding statistical tests are presented in Chapter 4. Because using these designs is often a very effective way to increase statistical power, it is worthwhile to look at them in more detail here.

Simple blocking. Table 6.1 depicts the case of a simple blocked design in which the treatment and control groups are each divided into males and females. In an analysis of variance format, the blocking variable (gender) becomes a "factor" with different "levels," (male and female) within which subjects are grouped. Each block or level is further subdivided, or crossed, with the independent variable (treatment vs. control conditions). The corresponding analysis of variance summary in Table 6.1 shows: the treatment main effect (G) which, of course, is the focus of the design; the main effect for blocks (B), which should be reasonably large for the blocking to be useful; the treatment by blocks interaction (G × B), which can be quite interesting if it is suspected that treatment has different effects on males versus females; and the residual or error (E) against which all effects are tested.

If we ignored the blocking factor in the design of Table 6.1 and simply tested the treatment versus control group difference using a one-way ANOVA or t-test for independent samples, the error term would be the pooled within-groups variance estimating the population variance common to the groups, σ^2. Analogously, σ would be the *ES* denominator for statistical power analysis. The ANOVA summary in Table 6.1 shows that, with the blocking factor, the error variance has been partitioned into estimates of three components, $\sigma_B^2 + \sigma_{GB}^2 + \sigma_E^2$, only the latter of which is used in the error term for significance testing. To the extent that there is much variance among blocks (σ_B^2) or interaction between blocks and treatment groups (σ_{GB}^2), therefore, the error term has decreased and the likelihood of statistical significance has increased. Correspondingly, the *ES* denominator should be σ_E, not σ. The term σ_E^2 is estimated by the variance within blocks within experimental groups. For our example, it would be the common (or pooled) variance from within four cells: males in treatment, males in control, females in treatment, and females in control. As we look at the variance within *only* the treatment population (or, alternatively, only the control population), it divides into two components—a within-blocks component (call it σ_w^2) and a between-blocks component (call it σ_b^2) so that the total $\sigma^2 = \sigma_w^2 + \sigma_b^2$.

In this formulation σ_w^2 corresponds to the σ_E^2 that will be the error term for significance testing and, in standard deviation form, the denominator of the *ES* appropriate to this design. The term σ_b^2 represents that variance within treatment (or control) populations that will contribute to the between-blocks component, σ_B^2, in the ANOVA design and to the interaction between groups and blocks, σ_{GB}^2, though the latter is not defined until treatment and control are compared (Kirk, 1982, sec. 8.6).

We can express the *ES* for a blocked ANOVA design directly, where σ_w^2 is the common (or pooled) within-blocks variance, as follows:

$$ES_{ab} = \frac{\mu_t - \mu_c}{\sigma_w}$$

To show the extent to which ES_{ab} is larger than ES_{ai} for the corresponding one-way ANOVA without the blocking factor, we note that, since $\sigma^2 = \sigma_w^2 + \sigma_b^2$, we can express ES_{ab} as follows:

$$ES_{ab} = \frac{\mu_t - \mu_c}{\sigma\sqrt{\sigma_w^2/(\sigma_w^2 + \sigma_b^2)}} = \frac{\mu_t - \mu_c}{\sigma\sqrt{1 - (\sigma_b^2/(\sigma_w^2 + \sigma_b^2))}}$$

The term $\sigma_b^2/(\sigma_w^2 + \sigma_b^2)$ is in the form of an intraclass correlation indicating the proportion of the total variance represented by the between-blocks variance. More particularly, following Hays (1973), it represents an intraclass correlation, ρ_i, when blocks are viewed as a random factor (arbitrary categories), and it represents Hays' omega squared coefficient, ω^2, when blocks are viewed as a fixed factor (nonarbitrary categories). Using PV_b to represent the general case of the proportion of variance accounted for by the blocking factor, we get:

$$ES_{ab} = \frac{\mu_t - \mu_c}{\sigma\sqrt{1 - PV_b}} = \frac{ES_{ai}}{\sqrt{1 - PV_b}}$$

Thus if we can estimate the proportion of within-groups variance attributable to differences among blocks, we can easily estimate the increase, $1/\sqrt{1 - PV_b}$, in ES when the blocked ANOVA is used in comparison to the unblocked ANOVA.

Note how considerably the effect size can be enhanced by reduction of variance through blocking. If a good blocking variable is chosen which, say, accounts for at least .56 of the within-group variance in the dependent measure, the effect size will be increased by 50%. For effect sizes that are modest to begin with, a 50% increase can boost statistical power by more than twice (see the power charts in Chapter 4). For reference, Table 6.2 shows the multiplier by which the unadjusted effect size is increased for various PV_b values (and some other adjustments to be discussed later). For PV_b below about .25, there is relatively little gain, but above that level the effect size is enhanced by worthwhile and progressively greater amounts.

It should be noted that more than one blocking variable can be used in this design. For the design of Table 6.1, for example, where subjects are

TABLE 6.2 Multiplier by Which *ES* Increases When a Blocking Variable, Covariate, or Paired Subjects Design Is Used to Reduce Within-Groups Variance

Proportion of variance associated with control variable*	Multiplier for ES increase
.05	1.03
.10	1.05
.15	1.08
.20	1.12
.25	1.15
.30	1.20
.35	1.24
.40	1.29
.45	1.35
.50	1.41
.55	1.49
.60	1.58
.65	1.69
.70	1.83
.75	2.00
.80	2.24
.85	2.58
.90	3.16
.95	4.47
.99	10.00

* PV_b for blocked ANOVA
r^2 for ANCOVA
r for paired subjects (assumed positive)

blocked according to gender, we could further divide each sex group according to, say, IQ (high vs. low). The error term for significance testing in this case is reduced by both the variance associated with the gender blocking and that associated with the IQ blocking. For statistical power determination, the effect size denominator is reduced correspondingly with a resulting increase in the overall effect size. There are some practical limits to the number of blocking factors that can be used in combination, however. First, additional blocking variables do not improve statistical power appreciably unless they are correlated with the dependent measure *and* relatively uncorrelated with the other blocking variables. That is, to be effective, each blocking variable must remove some new variance from the distribution of scores beyond what the other blocking factors are able to remove.

Second, each blocking variable reduces the number of degrees of freedom for the statistical test of the treatment effect by $j-1$ for the between-blocks component, plus another $j-1$ for the blocks by group interaction, where j is the number of levels (categories) into which subjects are blocked. Too many weak blocking variables could cost more power in lost degrees of freedom for significance testing than is gained through reduction of the within-groups variance.

A numerical example will not only illustrate further, but give some basis for comparing simple blocking with other designs to be discussed later. Table 6.3 displays some fictitious data for a comparison between a treatment and a control group with 26 subjects in each. The dependent measure for this case is a mathematics achievement test that has good reliability but shows relatively large variation among subjects, rather like the language measures used in the example in Chapter 5.

If we estimate the treatment ES for these data, ignoring the blocking factor, it is .33. We get this by differencing the means on the dependent measure ($80.9 - 77.0 = 3.9$) and dividing by the pooled within-group standard deviations ($\sqrt{(11.5^2 + 12.2^2)/2} = 11.9$). The corresponding statistical power (from the charts in Chapter 4) with $n = 26$ and $\alpha = .05$ is about .20, a modest value that gives little chance of detecting the effect. And, indeed, the F-ratio for this comparison is 1.42 ($df = 1,50$) which falls short of significance.

We know, however, that IQ is strongly related to mathematics ability and may decide that the natural differences among the subjects in IQ are not relevant to our assessment of treatment effects. We are more interested to know if the treatment produces an effect that is large relative to the variation in achievement scores for subjects at a given IQ level. Table 6.3 therefore also shows a simple blocking by "high" and "low" IQ.

If we estimate the ES for these data under these new assumptions, we divide the same numerator as before by a different denominator: the pooled standard deviations from each cell of the design, that is, high IQ treatment group, high IQ control group, low IQ treatment group, and low IQ control group ($\sqrt{(6.5^2 + 6.9^2 + 6.9^2 + 7.6^2)/4} = 7.0$). This results in an effect size estimate of .56, considerably larger than the .33 value from the unblocked design. For $n = 26$ and $\alpha = .05$, the statistical power (from the charts) is now about .50, more than double the value for the unblocked design. Moreover, the F-ratio for the treatment main effect is now 4.06 ($df = 1,48$) which is significant at $p = .05$ even though it is tested with two fewer degrees of freedom in its denominator. Furthermore, as a fringe benefit, we could get a test of the interaction between treatment and IQ, a test that will indicate if subjects with high IQ responded

TABLE 6.3 An Example of Analysis of a Two-Group Comparison on Achievement Test Scores (Ach) with IQ as a Blocking or Covariate Variable

	Treatment group			Control group			
	Subject	IQ	Ach	Subject	IQ	Ach	
	S1	76	61	S27	74	53	
	S2	79	62	S28	80	64	
Low IQ	S3	83	71	S29	84	59	
	S4	85	64	S30	85	65	
n = 13	S5	87	74	S31	89	63	n= 13
$\bar{X}$ = 71.7 (Ach)	S6	92	70	S32	90	70	$\bar{X}$ = 67.2 (Ach)
s.d. = 6.5	S7	92	74	S33	92	64	s.d. = 6.9
	S8	94	70	S34	92	74	
	S9	95	78	S35	93	69	
	S10	95	70	S36	97	73	
	S11	98	79	S37	98	71	
	S12	99	77	S38	100	79	
	S13	100	82	S39	101	70	
	S14	103	77	S40	101	78	
	S15	105	88	S41	104	77	
High IQ	S16	105	83	S42	107	83	
	S17	108	87	S43	108	77	
n = 13	S18	109	84	S44	110	88	n = 13
$\bar{X}$ = 90.2 (Ach)	S19	110	92	S45	110	83	$\bar{X}$ = 86.8 (Ach)
s.d. = 6.9	S20	113	85	S46	111	88	s.d. = 7.6
	S21	115	93	S47	113	85	
	S22	121	92	S48	119	94	
	S23	122	97	S49	123	85	
	S24	124	94	S50	123	95	
	S25	129	100	S51	132	96	
	S26	133	100	S52	135	100	
	n = 26			n = 26			
	$\bar{X}$ = 80.9 (Ach)			$\bar{X}$ = 77.0 (Ach)			
	s.d = 11.5			s.d. = 12.2			

differently to the treatment from the way in which subjects with low IQ responded.

Analysis of covariance. In the example above, the blocking by IQ is rather crude, categorizing subjects only into low and high groups. Since IQ is a continuous variable, it is reasonable to consider extending the blocking concept to finer groupings. We could, for example, block on each individual IQ value, one block for subjects with IQ = 85, one block for subjects with IQ = 86, and so forth. If we took this approach, however, we would soon run into difficulty. For one thing, we would need to have at least two subjects in every block (one treatment and one control) and, in any event, have the same number in each block to avoid difficulties with the ANOVA analysis. Sufficient subjects may not be available at each IQ level needed. Furthermore, this approach will be expensive in terms of degrees of freedom, $2(j - 1)$ of which are lost from the denominator of the F-test in the two-group blocked design.

Fortunately, there is an alternative to such fine-grained blocking that often has nearly the same effect on statistical power without placing demands on the distribution of IQ scores among subjects or using excessive degrees of freedom. That alternative is the analysis of covariance (ANCOVA). Rather than blocking on each individual value of a variable, ANCOVA regresses the study dependent variable upon the covariate variable. In this way, ANCOVA makes use of all the variability among subjects on the covariate without requiring that they be distributed evenly over each value of that variable. It substitutes a regression line for a set of blocks in cases where the blocking variable is continuous. Furthermore, it takes only one degree of freedom per covariate to fit the regression line. On the other hand, in accounting for the relationship between the covariate and the dependent variable, the ANCOVA includes only the linear component, whereas blocking has no such restriction. (For a more detailed comparison of blocking and ANCOVA, see Bonett, 1982, and Maxwell, Delaney, & Dill, 1984).

With regard to statistical power, ANCOVA, like blocking, yields considerable advantage in cases where there is large variability among subjects on the dependent measure of interest. To the extent that the covariate is correlated with the dependent measure, ANCOVA removes from subject heterogeneity that portion of the scores "predictable" by that covariate, leaving only the uncorrelated residuals to analyze for treatment versus control group differences. The *ES* denominator for ANCOVA, therefore, is not σ, the within-groups population standard deviation, but σ_r, the standard deviation for the residuals left when the covariate is partialed out. The corresponding effect size for one-way analysis of covariance (ES_{ac}), then, is as follows:

$$ES_{ac} = \frac{\mu_t - \mu_c}{\sigma_r}$$

As reported in Chapter 4, if we know the correlation between the covariate and the dependent variable, or the multiple correlation between a set of covariates and the dependent variable, it is easy to determine the effect ANCOVA will have upon statistical power in comparison to the analogous analysis without the covariate. As in the case of blocking, described above, we adjust the *ES* denominator to reflect the removal of that portion of the within-groups variance attributable to the control variable. Letting *r* be the correlation (or multiple correlation) between the covariate(s) and the dependent measure, the proportion of variance in the scores "controlled" by the covariate is r^2. We can represent this adjustment in relation to the effect size for the analogous one-way ANOVA without covariates (ES_{ai}) as follows:

$$ES_{ac} = \frac{\mu_t - \mu_c}{\sigma\sqrt{1 - r^2}} = \frac{ES_{ai}}{\sqrt{1 - r^2}}$$

For reference, Table 6.2 (presented earlier) shows the multiplier by which the unadjusted effect size is increased for various values of r^2, the squared correlation (or squared multiple correlation) between the covariate(s) and the dependent measure of interest.

Turning to the data of Table 6.3, we can illustrate the use of ANCOVA by recalculating the effect size and statistical power when IQ is treated as a covariate rather than as a blocking variable. The *ES* for that data based on a simple two-group comparison, recall, was .33 and, blocked on IQ, was .56. The correlation between IQ and the mathematics achievement dependent measure across all subjects is .94. For statistical power purposes, the effect size using ANCOVA on these data is now calculated at .96 (i.e., 3.9 / (11.9 $\sqrt{1 - .94^2}$)). Statistical power (from the charts in Chapter 4) with $n = 26$ and $\alpha = .05$, which was about .20 in the unadjusted case and .50 in the blocked design, has now risen to over .90, a considerable improvement. The F-ratio for the treatment main effect, in turn, is 12.16 ($df = 1,49$)—significant at well beyond the .01 level. The improvement the ANCOVA using IQ shows over blocking using the same IQ variable occurs because the ANCOVA took advantage of the full range of IQ variation, while the blocking only used the crude differentiation between high and low scores.

Pretest-posttest ANCOVA design. It might be worth saying a few words specifically about the common situation in treatment effectiveness research where both pretest and posttest values on the dependent measure are available. That is, dependent measures are collected in both the treatment and control group prior to treatment (pretest) and again subsequent to treatment (posttest). There are many good reasons for using the pretest-posttest design. For example, pretest scores allow subjects to be paired on pretest values prior to assignment to experimental groups to ensure initial equivalence on the dependent measure. Even if that cannot be done, they at least allow the treatment and control group to be compared for initial equivalence as a check on the adequacy of random assignment to experimental groups. Pretest scores also permit comparison of those that drop out of the treatment versus the control group prior to posttest to identify any differential attrition.

Of particular interest here, however, is the fact that the distribution of scores on the pretest measure carries a great deal of information about subject heterogeneity. In many cases of treatment effectiveness research, preexisting individual differences on the characteristic that treatment is intended to change will not be an appropriate standard for judging treatment effects. Of more relevance will be the size of the treatment effect relative to the dispersion of scores for subjects who began at the same initial or baseline level on that characteristic. In such situations, a pretest measure is an obvious candidate for use as a covariate in ANCOVA or, less powerfully, as a blocking factor in a blocked design. Since pretest-posttest correlations are generally high, often approaching the test-retest reliability of the measure, pretest as a covariate can dramatically increase the operative effect size in a treatment-control comparison. Table 6.2, presented earlier, shows that if the pretest correlates .80 or greater with the posttest ($r^2 = .64$), which is quite likely in many situations, the operative effect size will be no less than about 1.69 times as large as without the covariate adjustment.

This design, ANCOVA with pretest as the covariate, is so powerful and so readily attainable in most instances of treatment effectiveness research that it should be taken as the standard to be used routinely unless there are good reasons to the contrary. In some cases, it will be impossible to obtain a pretest measure or undesirable to use it as a covariate—for example, when the proper basis of comparison for differences between the means is judged to be unadjusted within-group variance. In other cases, alternative designs will be feasible that are even more powerful—for example, some applications of paired subjects or repeated measures designs (see below). Also, ANCOVA requires certain specialized statistical assumptions that may not always hold (see, Kirk, 1982, chap. 14). In many cases, however, the pretest-posttest ANCOVA will be both appropriate and more powerful than the attainable alternatives.

Paired subjects or repeated measures designs. Above, we saw that the analysis of covariance design could be thought of as a blocking design in which the blocks were defined with a very fine grain on a continuous covariate variable. Another variation on the concept of a blocked design is to think of blocking on a finer grain with regard to the number of subjects in each block. The advantages of blocking for variance control come from clustering similar subjects together and separating dissimilar clusters. As we try to get clusters of subjects who are more similar to each other, we get smaller clusters. For instance, if we block only on gender, we get two relatively large clusters. If we block further on IQ, we subdivide each of those large clusters into smaller ones, even more homogeneous, and so on.

The limiting case is a block size of two paired subjects, one in the treatment group and one in the control group, matched as closely as possible on a range of variables thought to be related to the dependent measure. One step further is to match a subject with himself or herself—who, after all, could be more similar to a person than the same person? In this case, we have what is often called the repeated measures design. Each subject receives both the control condition and the treatment condition, generally at different times and in random order, and the dependent measure is taken after each condition. This design is diagrammed in Table 6.4. In the paired subjects version, two similar persons are "yoked" and randomly assigned, one to the treatment and one to the control condition. In the repeated measures version, the same person appears in both conditions. The resulting data are analyzed either as a randomized block ANOVA or in correlated t-test format.

This design has some clear disadvantages. There is, for example, a loss of one degree of freedom for each block (pair of measures or pair of subjects). In the paired subjects version, it can be difficult to obtain satisfactory matches in sufficient numbers to complete the design, and to do so may require a more restrictive selection from the subject population than is desirable as a sampling strategy. The repeated measures version of the design, where each subject is his/her own control, is not appropriate for all treatments—for example, those of long duration, those with lasting effects, or those whose effects might be mimicked by natural maturation.

Nevertheless, there are advantages of statistical power to this design. The operative effect size (ES_{sp}) has as its denominator the pooled within-

TABLE 6.4 Schematic for Paired Subjects or Repeated Measures Design

Blocks or subjects	Conditions	
	Treatment	Control
1	x_{11}	x_{21}
2	x_{12}	x_{22}
3	x_{13}	x_{23}
4	x_{14}	x_{24}
5	x_{15}	x_{25}
.	.	.
.	.	.
.	.	.
.	.	.
n	x_{1n}	x_{2n}

x_{kn} is observation k for subject n in the repeated measures design and the observation for subject k in subject pair n in the paired subjects design.

ANOVA summary

Source	Associated variance component	df	MS	F
Condition (C)	σ_C^2	$k-1$	MS_C	MS_C/MS_E
Ss blocks (S)	σ_S^2	$n-1$	MS_S	MS_S/MS_E
Error (E)	$\sigma_E^2 + \sigma_{CS}^2$	$(n-1)(k-1)$	MS_E	

blocks variance, σ_w, that is, the variance between matched subjects or the same subject on repeated measures, and excludes all of the between-blocks variance, that is, the differences among different or unmatched subjects. In cases where there is moderate to substantial subject heterogeneity on the dependent variable within the treatment and control groups, this design can effectively partition much of that noise out of the denominator of the effect size. It assumes, instead, that the proper basis for assessing a treatment effect is its size relative to the variability that occurs for an individual subject from occasion to occasion or, for paired subjects, between substantially similar persons.

The effect size for the paired subjects or repeated measures design (ANOVA or t-test with dependent samples) can be expressed as follows:

$$ES_{ap} = \frac{\mu_t - \mu_c}{\sigma_w}$$

Since these designs are essentially based on blocking, it is of little surprise that this formulation corresponds to that of the blocked ANOVA discussed earlier. There are some important differences, however, that have to do with the fact that the control factor is not explicitly defined as a separate variable but, rather, is implicit in the pairing of subjects or observations. One implication of this, as the ANOVA summary in Table 6.4 shows, is that the blocks by group interaction cannot be tested; the analogous conditions by subjects variance, σ^2_{CS}, cannot be separated from the error variance σ^2_E.

A second implication of the lack of an explicit control variable shows up when we compare the effect size formulation for these designs with that for the analogous one-way ANOVA without paired observations (ES_{ai}). As in the previous instances, we find that the denominator of ES_{ai} must be adjusted to reflect the proportion of the within-groups variance removed by the control factor. Since the control is the pairing itself, however, the associated variance is that which is held in common by the two sets of correlated observations rather than that associated with a separate or external variable. The proportion of variance held in common in such a situation corresponds to r, the correlation between the paired observations, and not r^2 as was the case for the analysis of covariance (Ozer, 1985). We thus have the following relationship:

$$ES_{ap} = \frac{\mu_t - \mu_c}{\sigma\sqrt{1 - r}} = \frac{ES_{ai}}{\sqrt{1 - r}}$$

Since r in this case corresponds to a proportion of within-groups variance, just as PV_b and r^2 do in the previous designs, then Table 6.2, presented earlier, will show the increase in effect size that accompanies various values of the correlation between paired observations in this design (note, however, that negative r will decrease ES_{ap}). With repeated measures or close matching, the correlation between pairs can easily be .60 or greater. As Table 6.2 shows, such circumstances increase the operative effect size by 1.5 or more compared to its unadjusted value. For r reaching .90, the effect size can be tripled.

The advantages of the repeated measures design can be seen more concretely in the data of Table 6.3. To impose that design format, we rank-order each subject in each group (treatment or control) according to IQ score, and pair subjects to make—as nearly as possible—matches on IQ. For each pair of matched subjects, one is assigned to the treatment group, one to the control group. Note that the IQ scores in this design are used only for matching; they do not appear in the analysis itself. The correlation between the 26 achievement scores for the treatment group paired with the 26 scores for the matched control is $r = .87$. For statistical power purposes, the effect size estimate (.33 in the original simple two-group comparison) is now .91 (i.e., $3.9/(11.9 \sqrt{1 - .87})$). The corresponding power value from the charts in Chapter 4 for $n = 26$ and $\alpha = .05$ is about .90, a substantial increase over the .20 power in the unadjusted treatment versus control comparison and very nearly as good as the ANCOVA results (which made somewhat more fine-grained use of the IQ information).

Comparing the variance controlled designs. From the standpoint of statistical power, all three of the above designs work on a similar principle. Each tests statistical significance using an estimate of the standard error of the difference between means which excludes that portion of the variance associated with a control variable. Correspondingly, the effect size parameter represents the difference between the treatment and control group means in relation to the standard deviation of the uncontrolled portion of the scores. The rationale for using a variance controlled design is that the controlled portion of the variance represents differences among subjects that are not relevant to assessing the magnitude of the differences produced by treatment and which the researcher, therefore, would like to hold constant in the experiment. If those differences are difficult to control procedurally, the next best thing is to measure them and try to remove their contribution from the data statistically.

The three designs reviewed above differ only in the way they handle the control variable. The blocked design treats it as a set of categories that may have various patterns of relationship with the dependent measure (e.g., curvilinear). The analysis of covariance treats the control variable as continuous, but adjusts only for the linear relationship between it and the dependent measure. The paired subjects design controls for the similarity within pairs on the dependent measure, without requiring that the basis for that similarity be made explicit, and adjusts for the linear relationship across pairs.

For purposes of controlling subject heterogeneity in treatment effectiveness research, it is important to note that these designs are not mutually exclusive nor restricted to a single control variable. There are many variations and combinations possible and, within available degrees of freedom, any number of control variables that can be included. More detail on these matters can be found in textbooks on experimental design (see Kirk, 1982; Myers, 1979; Winer, 1971). For the treatment effectiveness researcher, rec-

TABLE 6.5 Approximate Sample Size per Experimental Group Needed to Attain Various Criterion Levels of Power for a Range of Effect Sizes at Alpha = .05

		Power Criterion	
Effect size	*.80*	*.90*	*.95*
.10	1570	2100	2600
.20	395	525	650
.30	175	235	290
.40	100	130	165
.50	65	85	105
.60	45	60	75
.70	35	45	55
.80	25	35	45
.90	20	30	35
1.00	20	25	30

ognizing when these approaches are needed and applying them effectively are essential to conducting research with significant power to detect treatment effects.

Sample Size

The discussion of statistical power parameters and calculations in Chapter 4 of this volume revealed two important features of sample size in experimental design that are worth reemphasizing. First, sample size is indeed important—virtually any desired level of power can be attained in any design simply by making the samples large enough. Perhaps more important to recognize, however, is the second fact of sample size. For the range in which most treatment effect sizes fall, the sample size needed to attain high power levels is often *much* larger than what is customary, or perhaps even possible, under most circumstances of research.

Table 6.5 provides a summary of information extracted from the power charts of Chapter 4 to show the sample size needed in each experimental group to attain various criterion power levels at $\alpha = .05$ for a range of effect sizes. For effect sizes under .5, a minimal power of .80 cannot be attained with any fewer than about 100 subjects in each group, that is, 200 total in a treatment versus control group comparison. Moreover, as the effect size we are attempting to detect drops below .5, the sample size requirements shoot up dramatically.

The implications for the design of treatment effectiveness research are relatively clear. In most circumstances, the first tactics a researcher should use to attain adequate statistical power are those that increase the effect size. Those tactics include measurement selection (Chapter 5), statistical control of variance (this chapter), and maintaining strength and integrity in the independent variable (Chapter 7). Only when these factors are fine-tuned to maximize the operative effect size will it generally be profitable to consider sample size. With a sufficiently large operative effect size, the researcher has a reasonably good prospect of finding that the sample size required for adequate power is within a range that can be practically attained.

Distribution of subjects. Other than the question of how many to use, the subject issue with the most practical importance may be their distribution across experimental conditions in a research design. The relationship between statistical power and sample size is based less on the total number of subjects involved than on the number in each group or cell within the design. This means that, with regard to statistical power, close attention must be paid to the effect of the number of groups over which subjects are distributed and the proportion of subjects within each group.

It is clear, for example, that to maximize statistical power with a limited number of subjects, they should be distributed into two groups designed to contrast with each other—for example, the "strongest" version of the treatment compared with a "no treatment" control. The same total number of subjects distributed in a multi-group design will generally have less power. Suppose, as an illustration, that 100 subjects are available to study a treatment that has an effect size of .5 in comparison to a control group. Distributed into two equal groups, 50 in the treatment group and 50 in the control group, the statistical power of the design at $\alpha = .05$ is about .70 (from the power charts in Chapter 4). Suppose, alternatively, that those same 100 subjects are distributed evenly across four experimental conditions—a no treatment control, a placebo control, a regular treatment condition, and an enhanced treatment condition. In this four-group design, the treatment main effect would be tested in a one-way analysis of variance with 25 subjects in each group. Statistical power in this situation can be determined using the tables in Cohen (1977, Chap. 8). Assuming the same effect size contrasting the aggregate treatment groups with the aggregate control groups, the statistical power for the appropriate F-test is .53, notably lower than the .70 attained when the 100 subjects were distributed into only two groups. Indeed, this power level is equivalent to what would be attained in a two-group design of $n = 33$ subjects in each group. Thus, in power terms, dividing the limited number of subjects into four groups instead of two groups has been less efficient, equivalent to throwing away 34 of the 100 subjects available.

A somewhat different issue of distribution of subjects arises under conditions of constraints on the number (or proportion) of available subjects that can be assigned to a given experimental condition. For example, the professional staff associated with a treatment are often reluctant, for ethical or practical reasons, to have subjects assigned to a no treatment control condition. The challenge for the researcher in such circumstances is to design for the minimal number of subjects in the undesirable group while still maintaining adequate power.

One useful approach is to use unequal sample sizes, assigning more subjects, say, to the treatment condition than to the control condition (or vice versa). The "extra" subjects in the treatment condition improve statistical power in comparison to a design with the same smaller number of subjects in both treatment and control conditions. The practical question with regard to statistical power is how small one group can be made given that the researcher is able to compensate by assigning a larger number of subjects to the other group.

With a fixed number of subjects, maximal statistical power is attained when they are divided equally into treatment and control groups. One approach to the question of unequal distribution is to start with the equal n case which yields acceptable statistical power under the circumstances of the research and then examine the combinations of smaller n in one group and larger n in the other group that will keep power constant.

So long as the populations from which the samples are drawn are of equal size and equal variance, the combinations of unequal sample size that maintain a given level of power can be approximated fairly easily. For the difference between the means of two experimental groups to be statistically significant, the confidence intervals around each must not overlap. The radius of a confidence interval is $zse(\bar{X})$ where z is the normal deviate corresponding to the desired alpha level (e.g., 1.96 for $\alpha = .05$), or the corresponding t value for small samples, and $se(\bar{X})$ is the standard error of the mean. If the confidence intervals around two means are not to overlap, the interval between those means, say $\bar{X}_1$ and $\bar{X}_2$, must therefore be greater than $zse(\bar{X}_1) + zse(\bar{X}_2)$. As we decrease the n in one group, its $se(\bar{X})$ will increase. To compensate, the $se(\bar{X})$ of the other group must decrease at least an equivalent amount so that the confidence intervals maintain their same probability of not overlapping. The question of unequal n in the two groups, therefore, is a question, first, of how small the n of one group can get without having its confidence interval include the other mean directly and, second, how large the n of the other group must be to reduce its confidence interval by at least the amount by which the first one is expected to increase.

If we begin with the equal n value for which there is adequate statistical power, given ES and alpha, we can let v be the factor of less than one by which we reduce the n of the group we want smaller, and u be the factor of more than one by which we increase the n of the other group to compensate. For example, if $v = .5$, we mean to reduce the n of the corresponding group by half of the value required for statistical power with equal n. We can then plug vn and un into the appropriate standard error formulas and determine how small we can let vn be and how large un will have to be to compensate. This procedure is easy to illustrate for the common case of continuous measures tested with a t-test, F-test, or the like.

The standard error of the mean for such measures is $se(\bar{X}) = \sigma/\sqrt{n}$, where σ is the population standard deviation (assumed equal for the two populations) and n is the sample size. To maintain the same probability of statistical significance (power) as the equal n case, we want $z\sigma/\sqrt{vn} - z\sigma/\sqrt{n} = z\sigma/\sqrt{n} - z\sigma/\sqrt{un}$. Being common to all terms, $z\sigma/\sqrt{n}$ drops out leaving $(1/\sqrt{v}) - 1 = 1 - (1/\sqrt{u})$. Solving for u in terms of v we get:

$$u = \frac{1}{(2 - 1/\sqrt{v})^2}$$

Note first that when $v = .25$, the denominator of the fraction in this expression becomes zero requiring u to be infinite. This is the point at which the confidence interval for the smaller group includes the mean of the other group so that no matter how small the $se(\bar{X})$ of the other group, statistical significance cannot be attained. Thus we discover the limiting case for unequal distribution of subjects: We cannot have fewer than one-fourth the required equal n value in the smaller group and maintain adequate statistical power no matter how much we increase the size of the other group.

Given $v > .25$, then, what values of u do we need, that is, what increases from the equal n value do we need in the other group, to maintain the same level of statistical power? Table 6.6 shows u as a function of v for values of v between .25 and 1.0. At $v = 1.0$, of course, $u = 1.0$, recreating the equal n scenario with which we started.

Table 6.6 shows that as v gets close to the limiting value of .25, the increase in the sample size of the other group must get very large to compensate. For example, at $v = .30$, that is, reducing one group to .3 of the

TABLE 6.6 Relationship of the Proportion (*v*) Used to Decrease One
Equal *n* Group to the Multiplier (*u*) by Which the Other Must
Be Increased to Maintain the Same Power

v	*u*
.25	∞
.30	33
.35	10
.40	5.7
.45	3.9
.50	2.9
.55	2.4
.60	2.0
.65	1.7
.70	1.5
.75	1.4
.80	1.3
.85	1.2
.90	1.1
.95	1.1
1.00	1.0

equal *n* value required, the other group must increase by about 33 times the equal *n* value. Thus if the equal *n* case required *n* = 100 in each sample, we could maintain the same power comparing a sample of 30 with a sample of 3300. At larger values of *v*, however, the disproportion is much less extreme. At *v* = .5, for instance, *u* is less than 3. For most purposes, this is a much more practical range. It means that a researcher requiring *n* = 100 in each sample could maintain the same power by reducing one group to 50 and increasing the other to 300. The total number of subjects, of course, has increased from 200 to 350, showing the inefficiency of unequal sample sizes. In circumstances where it is much less desirable to assign subjects to one condition than to the other, however, this loss of efficiency may be less important than the ability to minimize the exposure of subjects to the undesirable condition.

Alpha

Treatment effectiveness researchers frequently set alpha at a relatively stringent level—for example, no larger than .05—and then proceed with their research without recognizing that, in many practical applications, they have implicitly decided that it is acceptable for beta to be quite large, often greater than .50. Both Type I error (α) and Type II error (β) generally have important implications in the investigation of treatment effects. Type I error can mean that an ineffective or innocuous treatment is judged beneficial or, possibly, harmful while Type II error permits a truly effective treatment (or truly harmful one) to go undiscovered. Under these circumstances it will rarely be defensible for a researcher to be explicit about the acceptable risk for one type of error and silent about the second.

Ideally, explicit alpha and beta risk-levels would be set, in advance of a study, based on a rational analysis of the costs, benefits, and other relevant factors associated with the consequences of error of each type (see Cascio & Zedeck, 1983; Schneider & Darcy, 1984). If information for such an analysis is lacking, it may be necessary to resort to some convention (such as $\alpha = .05$) as a kind of default alternative to the proper situational analysis. We will look first at what might be a proper basis for establishing a convention in treatment effectiveness research, then examine rational analysis as a superior approach.

If error risk levels must be set according to some standard of commonly accepted practice, it should be a convention that maintains some balance between the risk of Type I and Type II error, not one exclusively concerned with alpha levels. For practical treatment effectiveness research, the situation is generally one in which *both* types of error are serious. Under these circumstances, the most straightforward approach is to *set alpha risk and beta risk equal unless there is a clear reason to do otherwise*. If we hold to the usual convention that alpha should be .05, therefore, we should design research so that beta will also be .05. If such high standards are not practical, then both alpha and beta should be relaxed to some less stringent level—for example, .10 or even .20. Given that .10 is already about as liberal an alpha level as ever appears in print in the social sciences, it is debatable whether relaxing as far as .20 is justified, and certainly quite debatable whether an even larger value can easily be defended. Note, however, that an alpha level of .20 still means that there is an 80% probability that the statistical conclusions of the research will be correct, given a truly ineffective treatment. Though low by conventional statistical standards, this is a high probability for many decisions in everyday life. One might be pleased to know that the probability of making the right decision was as high as 80% when considering a marriage partner, an investment, a new job, and so forth.

To provide some framework for considering the design issues related to the criterion levels of alpha and beta set by the researcher, Table 6.7 shows the required sample size per group for the basic two-group experimental design at various effect sizes under various equal levels of alpha (two-

TABLE 6.7 Approximate Sample Size for Each Group Needed to Attain Various Equal Levels of Alpha and Beta for a Range of Effect Sizes

	Level of alpha and beta ($\alpha = \beta$)			
Effect size	*.20*	*.10*	*.05*	*.01*
.10	900	1715	2600	4810
.20	225	430	650	1200
.30	100	190	290	535
.40	60	110	165	300
.50	35	70	105	195
.60	25	50	75	135
.70	20	35	55	100
.80	15	30	45	75
.90	10	25	35	60
1.00	10	20	30	50

tailed) and beta. It is noteworthy that maintaining relatively low levels of alpha and beta risk (e.g., .05 or below) requires either rather large effect sizes or rather large sample sizes. Since much treatment effectiveness research involves relatively modest effect sizes and sample sizes, a clear difficulty is presented. If neither effect size nor sample size can be increased sufficiently to maintain a low risk of error, the only remaining strategy— other than abandoning the research altogether—is to permit higher risk of error.

No matter how sensible, any general convention for setting error risk levels is, of necessity, rather crude. A better basis, when possible, is analysis of the relative consequences of Type I and Type II error for the specific treatment situation under investigation. Good advice on such analysis can be found in Brown (1983), Cascio and Zedeck (1983), Nagel and Neef (1977), and Schneider and Darcy (1984). In summary form, their advice is to consider the following points in setting error risk levels:

Prior probability. Since the null hypothesis is either true or false, only one type of inferential error is possible in a given study: Type I for a true null hypothesis and Type II for a false null hypothesis. The problem, of course, is that we do not know if the null hypothesis is true or false and thus do not know which type of error is relevant to our situation. When there is evidence that makes one alternative more likely, however, the associated error should be given more importance. If, for example, prior research tends to show a treatment effect, the researcher should be especially concerned about protection against Type II error and set beta accordingly.

Directionality of significance testing. A significance test of a one-tailed hypothesis (e.g., that the treatment group is superior to the control group) conducted at a given alpha level has higher power, that is, smaller beta, than a two-tailed test at the same alpha (e.g., that treatment is either superior *or* inferior to control). In treatment effectiveness research, concern often centers on one direction of effects: for instance, whether a new treatment is better than existing treatments. In these situations it is reasonable to argue that one-tailed tests are justified and that using two-tailed tests amounts to an inappropriate restriction of the alpha level.

Relative costs and benefits. Perhaps the most important aspect of error risk in treatment effectiveness research has to do with the consequences of error. Rarely will the costs of each type of error be the same nor will the benefits of each type of correct inference be the same. Sometimes treatment effects and their absence can be interpreted directly in terms of dollars saved or spent, lives saved or lost, and the like. In such cases it is relatively easy to work out the optimal relationship between alpha and beta error risk. Suppose, for example, that failing to apply a new, effective treatment to 100 patients would cause an additional 10 lives to be lost in comparison to conventional treatment and applying a new ineffective treatment in place of conventional treatment would cause an additional five lives to be lost. The relative cost of a Type II error in this case is twice as high a that of a Type I error. It follows that we should assume proportionately less risk of Type II error, and beta should be set at half alpha.

Often, however, the consequences of Type I and Type II error in treatment effectiveness research cannot be specified in such definite terms. The researcher must then rely on some judgment about the relative seriousness of the risks. This might be approached by asking those familiar with the treatment circumstances to rate the error risks and the degree of certainty that they feel is minimal for the conclusions of the research. For instance, such information may reveal that responsible persons knowledgeable about the context of the research feel, on average, that a 95% probability of detecting a meaningful effect is minimal and that Type II error is three times as serious as Type I. This indicates that beta should be set at .05 (power = .95) and alpha at .15. Nagel and Neef (1977) provide a useful decision theory approach to this judgment process that has the advantage of requiring relatively simple judgments from those whose values are relevant to the research context.

Conclusion

Statistical power in treatment effectiveness research is strongly influenced by decisions the researcher makes about certain crucial aspects of the research design. This chapter has discussed the ways in which power can be increased by including control variables in the design to reduce statistically the variability among subjects on the dependent measure, by optimally deploying subjects across experimental conditions, and by setting error risk levels on rational grounds rather than according to a narrow and one-sided convention.

7. The Independent Variable and the Role of Theory

The independent variable in treatment effectiveness research is defined by the treatment conditions to which subjects are exposed. It is generally a categorical variable reflecting molar group membership, rather than a graduated variable reflecting incremental differences in amount of treatment. In the two-group treatment versus control comparison, for example, the independent variable is a simple dichotomy which can be dummy coded with the value of, say, one for each subject in the treatment group and zero for each subject in the control group. What is generally important about it, therefore, is not its numerical value but the nature of the treatment that is actually applied to the subjects in each condition or, more specifically, the nature of the contrast between the treatments applied to different conditions.

The general relationship between the characteristics of the treatment and statistical power is readily apparent. For an effective treatment, the stronger it is relative to the control condition the larger the measured treatment effect should be. Larger treatment effects, in turn, increase the probability of attaining statistical significance and, hence, statistical power. Conversely, anything that degrades the treatment (or upgrades the control) will decrease the measured treatment effect and, with it, the statistical power.

Treatment effects show up in the conventional statistical models as constant positive or negative values that are added to the dependent variable scores of each subject in each respective group. If, for example, we have an untreated control population with a mean score on the Peabody Picture Vocabulary test of 100, we suppose that a given treatment adds some constant value, say 10 points, to each score, resulting in a treatment group mean of 110. Statistical analysis would test, on sample values, whether the difference between $\bar{X}_t = 110$ and $\bar{X}_c = 100$ was statistically significant. If the researcher designing the experiment could have strengthened the treatment manipulation somewhat so that the effect was 12 points instead of 10, that is, $\bar{X}_t = 112$ compared with $\bar{X}_c = 100$, the effect size numerator and, consequently the power, would have been larger (assuming the variances stayed constant).

Underlying the categorical group identification carried in the independent variable, therefore, is some contrast between two levels or "doses" of the treatment of interest and the different average effect they have on subjects in the respective groups. The particular treatment levels represented in the research can make a great deal of difference to the outcome, both statistical and practical.

Dose-response functions. Experimental design is based on the premise that treatment levels can be made to vary and that different levels might result in different responses. Something that cannot ordinarily be varied, like gravity, cannot be used as an experimental treatment—we have no way to set up a contrast, for example, between a "treatment" with gravity and a "control" without gravity. One way to represent the relationship between treatment level and response is the dose-response function, a plotting of the response on a particular dependent variable as a function of the treatment dose. Figure 7.1 illustrates a dose-response function for the relationship between psychotherapy outcome and the number of sessions. Treatment effectiveness research can be represented on the dose-response function as a selection of two or more treatment levels, (one of which may be no treatment) to be contrasted on the dependent measure. The difference between the average effects of the selected treatment levels, shown as Δ in Figure 7.1, corresponds to the treatment constant that appears in the statistical models for experimental research and to the numerator of the effect size parameter. If the researcher does not know the shape of the underlying dose-response function, which is usually the case, great care must be made in selecting treatment levels and in making inferences from the results of only a few treatment level contrasts.

It is instructive to examine some of the general forms dose-response functions might have. The simplest is the step-function (Figure 7.2, panel A). For this case, a range of low doses produces the same low response on the dependent measure while anything higher produces a constant higher response. This function corresponds to global, molar types of treatments that come in all-or-nothing packages and have all-or-nothing effects. For example, an impacted tooth can be left in, producing a painful effect, or removed, which stops the pain. There are no in-between levels for this

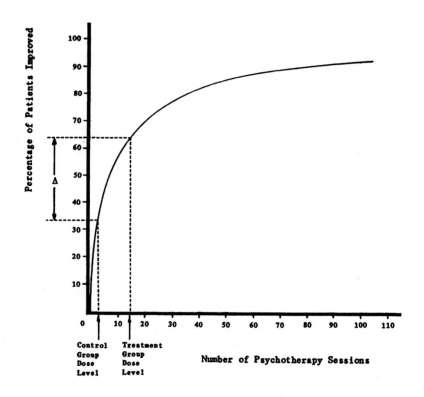

Source: Adapted from Howard et al., 1986

Figure 7.1: A Dose-Response Function for Psychotherapy

particular treatment—a tooth cannot be "a little bit extracted"—nor are there in-between levels for the response.

Relatively few treatments of interest in the behavioral sciences are of this global, molar all or nothing sort. It is worth observing, however, that this type of treatment has the dose-response function most closely aligned with the typical treatment versus control treatment effectiveness study. Only for this case does the simple dichotomous independent variable correspond well with the underlying dose-response function. For this relationship the mean treatment-control contrast will be a constant so long as the control group receives a dose below threshold and the treatment group re-

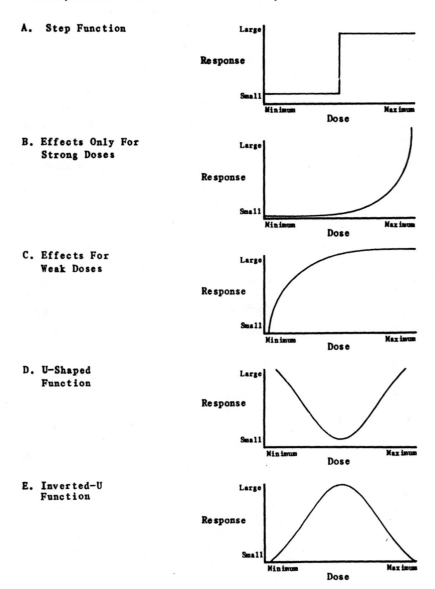

Figure 7.2: Some Different Possible Forms for Dose-Response Functions

ceives a dose above threshold. Moreover, the size of that increment will not generally be altered by variations among subjects in the dose actually received in a single study nor by variations among researchers in the doses selected for different studies.

Unfortunately, there is no reason to believe that step-functions are typical of the dose-response relationships for treatments in the behavioral sciences. For the range of functions more likely in such research, the particular treatment levels chosen by the researcher to compare can make a great difference in the outcome. Consider, for example, the dose-response curves shown in the remaining panels of Figure 7.2. Panel B shows a relationship in which there are effects only for a relatively strong treatment (e.g., perhaps psychotherapy with hardened criminals). If the researcher selects a weak treatment level to compare with, say, a no treatment control, little effect will be found. This could erroneously lead to the conclusion that the treatment is categorically ineffective when, in fact, it is quite effective at higher doses.

Alternatively, panel C shows a pattern in which very small doses of the treatment have relatively large effects (e.g., perhaps exposure to toxins). The challenge to the research in this case has more to do with the control group. Clearly, any contamination of the controls, even a weak dose of the treatment under investigation, will sharply reduce the contrast between treatment and control conditions and make treatment effects more difficult to detect. Panels D and E show other possible, though relatively unlikely, dose-response functions. Such U functions and inverted U functions, when they occur, make the choice of treatment levels to study even more important. With a function like that in panel E, for example, a researcher could pick a low dose and a high dose to compare with a no treatment control and find no important differences, completely missing the large effects that occur at intermediate doses.

A further complication is that the strength of many treatments of interest in social science research cannot be adequately expressed as a unidimensional dosage continuum. What, for example, is the dosage continuum for a high school mathematics curriculum? There surely are stronger and weaker versions of any curriculum, but its net strength is a function of many parameters–teacher quality, class size, amount of audio-visual support, and so forth. While we can continue to think in terms of a dose-response function for such a treatment, dosage is clearly a multidimensional variable. In these cases, treatment effects will vary with the strength of each separate treatment dimension or, more generally, with some function combining those dimensions in possibly complex ways to represent their conjoint action. The result, of course, is that there are numerous aspects of the treatment which, if not properly operationalized in a research study, may attenuate the effects and make them more difficult to detect.

Dose-response issues make for a kind of catch-22 situation in treatment effectiveness research. Such research is conducted to learn about the effects of a given treatment in a context where often little is already known. But, without some knowledge of the dose-response function, it is difficult to operationalize a treatment at a sufficient strength for the researcher to have some reasonable assurance that any effects produced will be large enough to detect with the methods available. Any single treatment effectiveness study for which there is no prior information about treatment effects or dose-response relations, therefore, will be something of a shot in the dark. It may or may not find anything and, in either event, the meaning of the results will be ambiguous.

How, then, can a researcher select an operationalization of an independent variable that will provide a reasonable likelihood that detectable effects will be produced if, in fact, the treatment of interest is capable of producing effects? More to the point, how can such an operationalization be made in the absence of knowledge about the dose-response function? In general, there are two strategies the researcher might follow and one to avoid. The one to avoid is to ignore dose-response issues and select a treatment operationalization haphazardly with no sense of its likely strength relative to alternative operationalizations. The two, more desirable strategies might be called "optimizing" and "parameterizing."

Optimizing the strength of the treatment operationalized in the research means defining that treatment in a context that provides some basis for judging what might constitute the optimal configuration for producing the expected effects. While there may be insufficient research directly on the treatment of interest (else why do the research) there are other sources of information that can be used to select a treatment sufficiently strong to have potentially detectable effects. One source, for example, is the experience and intuition of practitioners in the domain where the treatment, or variants on it, is applied. Their judgments of the strength and likelihood of effects from various operationalizations of the treatment may be a guide to selecting one worth consideration.

There may also be previous research on similar treatments or other treatments that share important elements with the treatment under consideration that can provide some basis for defining a treatment with sufficient strength to be worth testing. The strongest context for this approach is where programmatic research has been undertaken upon a treatment or a general treatment area so that there is a history of study from which to judge how a new variant should be operationalized (e.g., Wang & Walberg, 1983). In most cases, however, the researcher is extrapolating beyond existing knowledge when attempting to operationalize a treatment so that its effects can be measured.

What permits such extrapolation is some treatment theory, whether implicit or explicit, that helps identify the essential ingredients of treatment, the dosage level at which effects are likely, and the implementation that delivers it effectively. Thus whether based on practitioners' experience or previous research, some conceptual framework must be developed. It is this conceptual framework or treatment theory that becomes the basis for selecting an optimal treatment operationalization and the context for assessing its strength. The role of treatment theory, however rudimentary, is very important in treatment effectiveness research, especially with regard to designing studies in such a way that effects are produced, if possible, and those effects are detected. More will be said about treatment theory in the latter part of this chapter.

When there is little in the way of previous research, practice, or theory to go on, or when the researcher wishes to make a systematic investigation of the dose-response function, the appropriate strategy is a parametric study of different levels of treatment strength. In this approach, some treatment aspect is operationalized at different strengths so that differential effects can be detected. For example, treatment groups in a study might be assigned randomly so that one group receives five weeks of psychotherapy, one group ten weeks, one twenty, and so forth. Alternatively, if dose is thought to have more to do with the skill of the psychotherapist, groups may be compared in which treatment is provided by therapists of differing amounts of training and experience.

Note that there are many possible features of a treatment that can be varied, especially in complex treatments that have many elements and no obvious unidimensional dosage continuum. To highlight the elements that might be most influential in the treatment and those most appropriate to vary, some conceptual framework is, once again, essential. Unlike the optimizing strategy, however, in which no systematic comparisons of treatment variations are made, the parameterizing strategy can be used with very little prior knowledge. Given sufficient time and resources for research, study could be made of the effects of varying all treatment components identifiable within the conceptual framework adopted–a process that would be tedious but quite likely effective. This, in fact, is how dose-response curves are constructed once the important treatment elements are discovered.

From the standpoint of statistical power, one tradeoff must be noted in parametric studies of treatment variants. They necessarily require multiple treatment groups to represent the various levels under investigation. This means that a large number of subjects are required if the design is to maintain adequate power. As noted in Chapter 6, when there are low limits on the number of subjects available, power is greater if they are distributed into a single treatment group receiving a strong dose of treatment and a single control group receiving no treatment.

The Response Part of Dose-Response

Chapter 5 of this book reviewed a variety of issues that pertain to the measurement properties of dependent variables and their relationship with statistical power. Another set of issues involving dependent measures pertains to their relationship to the treatment or independent variable, and also has an influence on statistical power. Of particular concern in this regard are the nature of the dependent variable construct, the timing of its measurement, and its position in the causal chain induced by treatment.

Construct specification. To approach the issue of the dependent variable construct, consider the question of just what effects the treatment is expected to have. We can imagine a universe of states, traits, behaviors, and the like that characterize the recipients of any treatment. We can also imagine that any treatment, no matter how trivial, will have some effect on some of those characteristics and no effect on others. It follows that there will be larger or smaller effects to detect in a treatment effectiveness study depending upon the selection of dependent variable constructs to measure.

On what basis, therefore, should the researcher select dependent variables for treatment effectiveness research? If statistical power were the only consideration, the answer would be obvious. Dependent variables would be chosen to represent those constructs on which treatment is expected to induce the greatest change. The only way in which such constructs can be identified is through a close examination of the treatment concept, the causal process it is presumed to induce, and the particulars of the operationalization chosen for a specific study. Sometimes there is prior research and theory to bear on these issues; sometimes they must be judged from original analysis of the treatment. In either event, the question of what dependent variable constructs will show the greatest effects is very closely linked with the question of the nature of treatment and treatment processes.

There are, of course, other considerations besides sheer effect size and statistical power in selecting dependent variables for treatment effectiveness research. In some cases there is only one dependent variable that is of any interest, and the entire point of investigating treatments may be to find those that affect that one variable. For example, in a medical context the only outcome of much interest for treatment for a universally fatal condition might be whether it affects the mortality rate. Or, treatments provided to identified juvenile delinquents may be viewed exclusively in terms of their effects on delinquency.

In such cases, the universe from which dependent variables are chosen is a very small one, but there are still important choices to be made. There are, for example, several variants on the construct of juvenile delinquency. Official delinquency refers to legally chargeable acts that come to the attention of law enforcement authorities. Behavioral delinquency, on the other hand, includes such acts whether or not they come to the attention of the authorities. The construct of antisocial behavior, moreover, encompasses behavior that threatens persons, property, or self whether or not it happens to be illegal. Any given study of treatment for delinquents might be concerned with different aspects of these constructs. Furthermore, any given treatment may affect some of these constructs more than others. Even in this restricted construct domain, therefore, the selection of a dependent variable appropriate to the treatment is not a trivial issue and may have important implications for the nature and size of the measured effects found in a study.

In other situations there may be much less prior definition of the constructs that treatment is expected to affect or, indeed, even of the constructs it is desirable to affect. Psychotherapy, for example, is a treatment that is often intended to have effects over a potentially broad range of patients' emotions, cognitions, and behavior. In addition, even if treatment were targeted on a specific condition, say depression, it might still be a matter of considerable interest if there were other unanticipated benefits. For instance, treatment might improve social relations or result in fewer days of absence from work even if there were no measurable effects on depression as an emotional state. And, of course, a construct as general as depression admits to many operational variants, much like that of delinquency described earlier. In cases such as these the selection of dependent variables is a complex affair. Two researchers might make very different selections and, even given apparently similar selections, might find that treatment produced effects of very different magnitude on the respective dependent variables they had chosen.

Timing. With dependent variable constructs that appropriately reflect the domain in which treatment can be expected to have effects and operational measures of those constructs, the results may still depend upon the timing of measurement (Kelly & McGrath, 1988). A given dose of treatment, no matter how strong, does not necessarily produce an immediate, constant, and enduring effect. The effect may be delayed, may build slowly, or may peak and then diminish. We can represent treatment effects as a function of time with a decay function such as those shown in Figure 7.3. Since some effects may begin shortly after the onset of treatment, we plot effects on a given dependent variable from the time the treatment begins.

Panel A in Figure 7.3 shows the treatment-effect decay function that seems to be assumed in many treatment effectiveness studies that pay no particular attention to the timing of dependent measures. The treatment effect appears at full strength immediately at the conclusion of treatment and continues undiminished for some relatively long period thereafter. Under such circumstances, the size of the measured effect subsequent to treatment is virtually the same no matter when it is measured. Panel B, by comparison, shows a "sleeper effect" or delayed effect. In this case, the effect is very small at the conclusion of treatment and peaks at some later time. Clearly if the dependent variable is measured immediately after treatment, the effect size to be detected will be much smaller than at a later time.

Further complicating the question of the timing of treatment effects is the possibility that the timing could be different for different effects. Many treatment effectiveness studies use multiple dependent variables to detect effects on a variety of constructs. There is no necessity that the decay function for effects on each of these constructs be the same. A patient education program to increase compliance with medical advice, for example, might produce effects on patients' motivation that develop quickly and then decay (such as those in panel C of Figure 7.3). The effects on attitude toward compliance, however, might build more slowly but drop off less sharply (e.g., as in panel D) while the behavioral effects might show a still different pattern.

The implications of treatment-effect decay functions for research are apparent. The effect size to be detected by the research is not necessarily a

A. Immediate Effect,
   No Decay

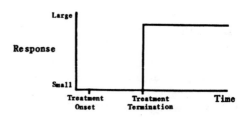

B. Delayed
   Effect

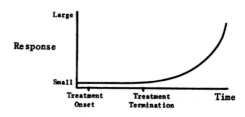

C. Immediate Effect,
   Rapid Decay

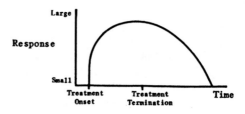

D. Early Effect,
   Slow Decay

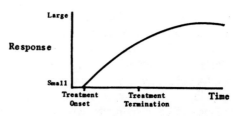

Figure 7.3: Some Different Possible Forms for Treatment-Effect Decay Functions

constant, but may vary according to the time at which it is measured. The researcher who wants to understand the decay function will need to make a series of measures at different times in order to discover its general shape. The researcher who wants to optimize statistical power should choose the time of measurement to coincide as closely as possible with the peak of the decay function so that the effect to be detected is at its maximum. This, of course, requires knowledge or good guesswork about the shape of the decay function–another catch-22 for treatment effectiveness research that cannot be easily resolved in the context of a single treatment study.

Proximal and distal effects. Treatment effectiveness research has to do with the study of cause-and-effect linkages. In the simplest case, the treatment is a direct and immediate cause of the effect of interest. For example, an elementary school teacher's instruction may result directly in improvements in the skill of students in doing long division. In other cases, however, the causal chain between the treatment and the effect of primary interest is longer. A juvenile delinquency prevention program may provide academic tutoring as a treatment in the belief that this helps juveniles succeed in school which, in turn, increases their skills and self-esteem which, in turn, makes it easier for them to adopt conventional social roles which, in turn, reduces the likelihood that they will be involved in delinquency. In such a causal chain, some effects occur earlier and are thus more proximal to the treatment, and others occur later and are more distal (see Judd & Kenny, 1981).

The importance of the position of a given effect in the causal chain to statistical power has to do with the possibility of slippage in the connection from one link to the next. Treatment effectiveness research is essentially a study of the covariation between the treatment independent variable and the dependent variable that indexes the effect of interest. At each link in a long causal chain there is the possibility of extraneous influences that dilute the strength of the connection with the next link. Academic tutoring may play a fairly direct role in helping juveniles succeed in school, but there are other factors that keep the relationship from being perfect–for example, the juvenile's personality and intelligence. Moreover, success in school may enhance skills and self-esteem, but there are other factors that intrude on the relationship, such as peer relations and family support. If we represent the covariation between treatment condition and outcome at successive links in the causal chain as correlations, beginning with the most proximal effect and moving through the chain to the dependent variable of primary interest, the result of the various extraneous influences at each point is to make the correlation less than perfect–that is, less than one.

Suppose for this juvenile delinquency example that the correlations at each step in the chain are presumed to be uniformly .80 at each link. The effect size relevant to statistical power can be represented as the correlation between the independent variable and the dependent variable of interest. If we let each effect in the causal chain be the dependent variable in its turn, it is easy to calculate the successive correlations with the independent variable. The correlation between any two variables in such a chain is simply the product of the correlation coefficients for all the intervening steps. Thus the correlation of the independent variable with school success is .80, with self-esteem is .64, with social roles is .51, and with delinquency is .41. With each step in the causal chain we find a diminishing effect size.

Since we have discussed effect sizes chiefly in terms of the standardized difference between treatment and control group means (*ES*), it is more instructive to transform the above correlations into that form. Table 7.1 shows the effect size for each successive step in a causal chain where we assume uniform correlations between the links of a given value. There is no necessity for the correlations between links to be uniform, of course, but this chart serves to illustrate the order of magnitude of the effect-size shrinkage under various general circumstances.

As Table 7.1 shows, even with a relatively high correlation at each successive link in the causal chain, the effect size to be detected in the research drops off noticeably from proximal effects to more distal ones. With lower correlations at each link, *ES* drops off so sharply as to be virtually undetectable after a few steps. One solution to the problem of diminishing effect sizes is to compensate for the corresponding loss of statistical power by making appropriate adjustments to the within-groups variance, sample size, or alpha level used in the research. Another approach is to measure all the variables intervening between the treatment and the effect of primary interest and apply a statistical significance test, not to each bivariate treatment-effect relationship, but to the entire causal model including all of the intervening steps (see Hunter, 1987).

Variable treatment delivery and response. As noted earlier, conventional statistical models for experimental research assume a constant, additive effect for each subject in each condition. This implies that each subject in the treatment condition receives the same dose of treatment and each subject in the control condition receives the same nondose. It also implies that with a given treatment dose each subject responds with the same effect. In many treatment applications, both these assumptions may well be false. We will look first at the matter of providing a constant dose of treatment, what Yeaton and Sechrest (1981) call treatment integrity, and then at the matter of subjects' responses to treatment.

The integrity of a treatment is the degree to which it is delivered as planned and, in particular, the degree to which it is delivered in a uniform manner in the right amounts to the right subjects at the right time. At one

TABLE 7.1 Effect Sizes (*ES*) for Effects at Successive Points Distal from the Treatment in a Causal Chain

Successive effects in the causal chain		Uniform correlation between links								
		.10	.20	.30	.40	.50	.60	.70	.80	.90
Most	E1	.20	.41	.63	.87	1.15	1.50	1.97	2.67	4.09
proximal	E2	.02	.08	.18	.32	.52	.77	1.13	1.66	2.75
	E3	.00	.02	.06	.12	.26	.45	.72	1.19	2.15
	E4	.00	.00	.02	.06	.12	.26	.49	.90	1.76
	E5	.00	.00	.00	.02	.06	.16	.34	.70	1.46
	E6	.00	.00	.00	.00	.04	.10	.24	.54	1.25
	E7	.00	.00	.00	.00	.02	.06	.16	.43	1.09
	E8	.00	.00	.00	.00	.00	.04	.12	.34	.96
Most	E9	.00	.00	.00	.00	.00	.02	.08	.26	.85
Distal	E10	.00	.00	.00	.00	.00	.02	.03	.22	.75

end of the continuum, we might consider the case of treatment effectiveness research conducted under tightly controlled clinical or laboratory conditions in which treatment delivery can be regulated very closely. Furthermore, we might first consider the case of a treatment that consists of a relatively fixed, easily determined dosage administered on only one occasion (e.g., taking a pill). Under these conditions we would expect a high degree of treatment integrity, delivery of a constant dose of treatment to each subject (or control, as appropriate), and, if the treatment has effects, relatively constant response from subject to subject within the same condition.

Treatment effectiveness research, however, cannot always be conducted under such carefully regulated circumstances. It must often be done in the field with voluntary subjects whose compliance with the treatment regimen is difficult to ensure. Moreover, the treatments of interest, especially in such conditions, are often not those for which dosage is easily determined and monitored nor are they necessarily delivered uniformly nor on a single occasion. The result is that the subjects in a treatment group may receive widely different amounts and even kinds of treatment (e.g., different mixes of components). If subjects' response to treatment varies with its amount and kind, then it follows that there will not be the constant increment added to each dependent variable score assumed in the statistical models. Moreover, under circumstances where treatment conditions cannot be kept uniform, it may also be difficult to keep control conditions uniform. When control subjects receive and respond to unintended doses of the research treatment or alternate treatment elsewhere, they also will not have a constant increment (often assumed zero) added to their scores.

When statistical analysis is done comparing treatment and control groups, all that registers as a treatment effect is the difference between the control group's mean response and the treatment group's mean response. If there is variation around those means it goes into the within-groups variance of the effect size denominator, making the overall *ES* smaller.

Maintaining a uniform application of treatment and control conditions is the best way to prevent this problem. Failing that, some diagnosis might be possible by comparing the variances of the individual experimental groups to identify any notably larger than the others. If *all* experimental groups have experienced inconsistent conditions, it may be possible to compare variances from the research with those in normative or archival data and thus still detect any excessive inflation.

Perhaps the best safeguard is for the researcher to actually measure the amount of treatment received by each subject in the treatment and control conditions. This technique not only yields information about how much variability there actually was, but provides some basis for statistical correction. Under some circumstances it might be possible to use such measures *separately* within each experimental group as a covariate to partial out of the scores some of the variance introduced by inconsistent treatment application. Alternatively, the treatment measure itself might be used as the independent variable in place of the usual group dichotomy. This will often increase power (Cook & Poole, 1982) but should be done cautiously since it may also introduce bias into the experimental comparison since subjects will not be randomly assigned to the different treatment levels (Mark, 1983).

So far in this discussion we have assumed that each subject responds the same way to treatment and that variation in response is introduced by way of varying amounts of treatment. We must also consider the possibility that different subjects will react differently to treatment, even to exactly the same treatment. This circumstance also adds to the variability on the dependent measures without making any compensating contribution to the contrast between the means of the different experimental groups. Differential response to treatment is especially likely for complex psychological, behavioral, and educational treatments, especially if extended over a relatively long time. For example, patients' reactions to long-term psychotherapy are likely to vary considerably depending on their personality, life history, and so forth.

This problem cannot be prevented simply through more consistent procedures and better experimental control as can the problem of inconsistent application of experimental conditions. Some statistical control is possible, however, if the researcher has some knowledge of the characteristics that differentiate subjects who will respond differently. Each such characteristic can be used as a blocking factor or covariate to remove from the *ES* denominator that variation in response associated with it. For example, if we know that more educated and less educated people are likely to react quite differently to treatment, we can block subjects by education before assigning them to experimental conditions or use education as a covariate in an analysis of covariance. As shown in Chapter 6, these techniques will statistically adjust for variance associated with the control variable and its interaction with experimental conditions.

Control Group Contrast

Not all aspects of the relationship between the independent variable and the effect size have to do primarily with the treatment. The choice of a control condition also plays an important role. The contrast between the treatment and control means can be heightened or diminished by choosing a control condition that is more or less different from the treatment condition in its expected effects upon the dependent measure. While there are many kinds of control conditions for various specialized purposes, the central comparison usually involves a treatment contrasted with one of the following four types of control:

No treatment control. In this control condition subjects receive virtually no treatment for the problem or situation that is of interest to the researcher. For example, speech therapy for stuttering might be assessed against a control condition in which subjects went about their normal lives with no treatment of any sort. This control condition can usually be expected to provide the greatest contrast with treatment and to offer the best opportunity for treatment to demonstrate its efficacy. For some situations, however, it may be very unrepresentative of subjects' experiences or be unethical. This occurs particularly for problems that do not normally go untreated–for example, severe illness.

Treatment as usual control. Some treatments are applied for specific purposes within a general context of a program that supports or surrounds that treatment. For example, a special vocational counseling component might be added to the services offered students in high school. Or, intensive supervision might be provided to a subset of juvenile delinquents on probation. Under such circumstances what is often arranged is a control group that receives the usual services for comparison with a treatment group that receives the usual services plus the special services. This contrast will not generally be as extreme as a true no treatment control–for example, a comparison with high school students assigned to a "no school" condition or delinquents assigned to a "no probation" condition. These control conditions are generally chosen for research within institutional contexts where, for the subjects of interest, there is no realistic alternative to being in that setting.

Placebo controls. The placebo control condition is one with a rather specialized function that is nonetheless widely used. It has its origins in medical research where it is important to distinguish the effects of a specific medical technique—for example, surgery or chemotherapy—from the nonspecific effects of patients' expectations and beliefs associated with treatment. This is an issue because of widespread evidence that those expectations and beliefs themselves have positive effects on many medical problems. More generally, the placebo control is used to isolate the effects of a particular "active ingredient" of interest from other treatment ingredients that naturally accompany it. For example, a researcher might suspect that self-disclosure by therapists (talking about their own feelings, etc.) plays an important role in the effects of psychotherapy. A treatment in which there was a high level of self-disclosure might then be arranged and compared with a placebo control in which all the usual elements of psychotherapy were present except for self-disclosure.

By definition, placebo conditions are quite similar to the treatments for which they serve as controls. It follows that placebo controls will generally show less contrast than, say, no treatment controls in treatment effectiveness research. This is particularly true when the active ingredient of interest in the treatment is very similar to the ingredients of a placebo–for example, when it also involves subjects' expectancies and beliefs. Thus the contrast will be larger for physical and chemical treatments in medicine than, say, for the interactional treatments of psychotherapy (Wilkins, 1986). Since placebo conditions are usually unrepresentative of any real treatment that might be provided, it can be argued that their value is mostly for theoretical purposes, distinguishing active from inactive treatment ingredients, and not as a representative of a practical alternative to the treatment of interest.

Alternate treatment control. In some cases the control condition is not so much a control as it is a legitimate alternative treatment. Thus traditional psychotherapy for phobias might be compared with behavior modification; drug therapy might be compared with bypass surgery for stroke patients, and so forth. Usually, but not always, the focus of interest is on one of the treatments in comparison to the other–for example, one is an innovation and the other is the traditional treatment. While different treatments may vary considerably in their effects, the contrast between alternate treatments can nonetheless generally be expected to be smaller than between treatment and no treatment. Indeed, to get any contrast at all, one treatment must be at least modestly better than the other. A lack of contrast, that is, a null result, can occur because both are ineffective or because both are equally effective (or, of course, because of low power in the comparison). Alternate treatment controls are most applicable when one of the treatments is already known to be effective and the practical issue of research interest is whether the alternative is better still.

The four types of control conditions described above are listed in approximate order according to the magnitude of the contrast they would generally be expected to show when compared with an effective treatment. The researcher's choice of a control group, therefore, will influence the size of the potential contrast and hence of the potential effect that appears in a study. Selection of the control group likely to show the greatest contrast from among those appropriate to the research issues can, therefore, have an important bearing on the statistical power of the design.

The Role of Theory

Where simple, discrete treatments are expected to yield readily observable effects of an easily specified sort, trial-and-error experimentation might be quite satisfactory. To determine if a newly discovered acid will dissolve gold, we need only drop in the gold and observe the results. With more complex treatments for more complex problems, however, detecting effects is not so easy. Especially with people problems (social, behavioral, and medical) we can anticipate uncertainty at every step of the way–in defining treatment, specifying dosage, anticipating and measuring its effects, and so forth.

This circumstance produces the kind of catch-22 for much treatment effectiveness research to which we alluded earlier. Catch-22 in Yossarian's tale, recall, was that to get out of the war you had to be certifiably insane, but anyone wanting to get out was obviously too sane to qualify. Catch-22 for the treatment effectiveness researcher is that you have to know a lot about the treatment and its effects to plan appropriate research on it, but it is to find out those very things that you want to do the research.

What is required in this kind of research is a sort of bootstrapping or iteration—using what is known to design research, the results of which increase what is known. As the observations in this chapter regarding the independent variable and power make clear, what holds that bootstrapping process together is some theoretical or conceptual framework about the nature of treatment and its effects. That framework is both the basis for research design and the vehicle that carries and integrates research results after they are produced (Bickman, 1987; Chen & Rossi, 1981; Lipsey, 1990).

In particular, for our purposes here, some theoretical or conceptual framework for treatment is essential for designing treatment effectiveness research with a good probability of actually detecting any true treatment effects. To conduct sensitive research the researcher must make decisions about treatment dose (strength), delivery (integrity), nature of effects, timing of effects, sequence of effects in the causal chain, subject interactions with treatment, sources of variability in dependent measures, and a host of other such matters. These decisions are not easy to make in a vacuum—the researcher must have, or develop, some framework for analysis and decision or risk a blind groping that is likely to yield erroneous and possibly misleading results.

One implication of this circumstance is that it will rarely be possible for a treatment effectiveness researcher to plunge right into the design of a study. Rather, it is to be expected that a certain amount of preliminary research will have to be done regarding the characteristics of candidate dependent measures, the implementation of treatment realistically capable of producing effects, the characteristics of target subject populations, and the like. A related implication is that little information of value will be gained from the one-shot treatment effectiveness study. Useful and credible results are more likely to flow from a program of research, whether by one or a number of researchers, in which systematic attention is paid to all aspects of the treatment and research circumstances. After all, bootstrapping and iteration only work effectively when the learning cycle repeats itself—not on a single pass.

Finally, a good word should be put in for qualitative study of treatment circumstances, subject populations, and related matters as a source of insight upon which to base more formal, quantitative treatment effectiveness research. When little is known about a treatment or program, much more is likely to be learned on the first go-around from interviews, observations, examinations of records and existing databases, and the like than from a crude, underpowered, and ill-informed comparative experiment with the error rates demonstrated in Chapter 1 of this volume.

8. Putting It All Together

This volume began with a challenge for researchers studying treatment effectiveness to design research with sufficient sensitivity to detect those effects they purport to investigate. Ample evidence indicates that conventional research practice, which generally neglects statistical power, yields an unacceptably high probability of Type II error.

The intervening chapters of this volume have been devoted to examining the nature of statistical power and the tactics by which it can be improved. In this final chapter we want to assemble those tactics into a strategy that might provide guidance to the treatment effectiveness researcher concerned about Type II error. Following that, it is worthwhile to consider some more general tactics that will help the field of treatment effectiveness research better manage its pervasive power problem.

Power Strategy

The discussion and analysis presented in this volume suggest four general steps for maximizing the sensitivity of research to treatment effects. The details of each appear in the preceding chapters. Here we will concentrate on how they might be sequenced and integrated.

Theory and concept. A coherent approach to statistical power in treatment effectiveness research actually begins with the issues discussed in Chapter 7 regarding the independent variable. The nature of the treatment versus control contrast set up in the research is fundamental to statistical power. If the research is worth doing, there should be some reason to expect that the treatment will have effects. The necessary basis for research design is a framework of concept and theory within which to make good guesses about just what to expect, when, and why.

The first element of such a framework is an operational notion of the strength of treatment required to have effects and how it can be consistently delivered. Following that must come some conception of what effects the treatment will have, at what time and at what place in the causal chain each effect might appear, and whether the treatment will have differential effects, that is, interact with the characteristics of the recipients.

The potential sources for such information are prior research and theory, the testimony of practitioners and treatment recipients, and close analysis of the proposed treatment and the problem context within which it is expected to work. The utility of this information is to guide the researcher in the operationalization of the independent variable (embracing both treatment and control conditions), specification of the outcome variables to be measured and the appropriate timing of measurement, and identification of any subject characteristics that may need to be measured to account for interactions with treatment. Coupled with considerations about internal validity, construct validity, and external validity in the research, this information provides the basis for the research design.

Measurement. Once some specification is made of the treatment effects that are expected, attention must turn to the operational issue of how to measure those effects. In many areas of treatment effectiveness research, especially those in which treatment effects might be subtle or complex, this is a much neglected issue. The dependent measures in treatment research constitute the listening stations for effects—if they are not pointed in the right direction, or not tuned to the right frequencies, or are too insensitive to register a meaningful signal, nothing will be heard even in the presence of loud voices.

The ideal measure for detecting treatment effects has no variability and responds markedly to a change in the characteristic it measures. Most measures that might be found ready-made or developed for research purposes are far from this ideal. Instead, candidate measures must generally be examined for, and often engineered for, the capability to respond to whatever level of change is of interest while maintaining minimal background noise variability. Their sensitivity to change or difference on the characteristic of interest can be examined via prior research, criterion contrast groups, and analysis of their intrinsic characteristics. Excessive variability can be investigated with reliability or generalizability studies, examination of correlations and distributions in existing research and databases, and the like. Whether for lack of responsiveness or excess variability, some attractive measures may have to be discarded; others will need modifications before they are satisfactory. Chapters 5 and 6 of this volume suggest various ways in which measures can be assessed and improved if necessary.

Note how theory and concept feed forward to the matter of operationalizing dependent measures. Not only is some level of theory essential for knowing what characteristics to measure, but it is useful for analyzing and modifying candidate measures as well. Measures most sensitive to treatment effects are those that focus specifically on what is new in subjects' responses, attitudes, behavior, status, and so forth after treatment. Theory can guide analysis of what new elements are expected to appear and thus help target the measures to the appropriate response domain.

Effect size. With sensitive measures and an outline for the research design, it is possible to ask the crucial question for statistical power—what threshold effect size should the research be designed to detect on each dependent measure? Under most research circumstances, that is, without massive numbers of available subjects and the funds to include them, this question must be answered before the research can be designed with some assurance that it will possess adequate sensitivity to the treatment effects under investigation.

On the surface this question seems relatively easy to answer—one merely determines the minimal *ES* that has practical or theoretical significance in the context of interest. In practice, however, this determination is often very difficult, which is no doubt one reason why there is so little discussion of this matter in the treatment effectiveness research literature. Part of the difficulty lies in judging just what constitutes practical or theoretical significance. In some situations this can be approached in formal decision-theory terms—for example, via cost-benefit analysis. In most situations, however, it must be approached more intuitively and be based, for example, on the researchers' or practitioners' judgment with, perhaps, some guidance from previous research or meta-analysis.

The process of turning judgments into statistical effect sizes can frequently be aided by some well-selected criterion contrasts of the sort discussed in Chapters 3 and 5. When researchers or practitioners can identify subject groups believed to differ by a meaningful amount on the characteristic that treatment is expected to affect, and the candidate dependent measures can be applied to them, or perhaps already have been, it is a simple matter to compute the equivalent *ES*.

The other part of the difficulty of deciding what minimal effect size the research should be capable of detecting is inherent in the nature of the concept of a statistical effect size itself. At root, it is a relativistic concept representing the treatment-control difference on a measure only in relation to the within-groups (or populations) variability on the measure. Since many factors beside the treatment impact influence both the numerator and denominator of the effect size parameter, its magnitude may bear no close relationship to the practical significance of an effect. Thus small statistical effects can correspond to large practical effects and vice versa.

This relativity makes it all the more important for the researcher to have a specific idea of the *ES* on a particular measure that it is desirable to be able to detect. Generally, the easiest figure to work with at this point is what might be called the "zero order" effect size. This is the *ES* value, in the customary standard deviation units, for the simple treatment-control contrast on a dependent measure without any adjustments, covariates, and the like. With this value in hand, the researcher is in a position to conduct a careful power analysis and design the subsequent research accordingly.

Power analysis. Power analysis consists of determining the statistical power that will obtain for various configurations of a statistical test, alpha level, sample size, and effect size. Its purpose is to guide the researcher to a research design that reaches whatever criterion power level is set. What that power criterion should be, of course, is up to the researcher. The advice of this volume (Chapter 6) is that it be set, along with alpha, according to the relative costs of Type II and Type I error or the relative benefits of avoiding those errors. If such an error risk analysis is not possible, it is recommended that the researcher set $\alpha = \beta$ when the potential treatment effects are of practical significance. This practice would at least ensure that the same emphasis be given to Type II error that is conventionally given to Type I.

With a criterion power level set, an alpha, and a threshold value for the zero-order *ES* to be detected, the researcher can proceed with a power analysis. The primary factors for consideration, in rough order of priority, are: 1) enhancing the operative *ES* to make the design as efficient as possible, 2) determining the necessary sample size, and 3) relaxing the error risk criteria (α and β) if necessary to accommodate limits on sample size or effect size.

Generally speaking, effect size enhancements are more cost-effective to engineer than are sample size increases. This is because much of what determines effect size has to do with the selection of measures, statistical analysis, treatment implementation, and other such issues that are intrinsic parts of the research in all circumstances. Determining how best to enhance *ES* requires some analysis and diagnosis of these factors for the particular research situation at hand. A tactic that can almost always be used to good effect, however, is variance control, both procedural and statistical. Procedural variance control means tight standardization of treatment and control conditions, sampling, and measurement. Statistical variance control uses covariates or blocking factors and other such techniques to separate variance judged irrelevant to the assessment of treatment effects from the error term for significance testing and, correspondingly, from the *ES* denominator (see Chapters 4 and 6). As shown earlier in this volume, such techniques can sometimes increase the operative *ES* two or threefold or more.

Once an estimate is made of the operative *ES* to be detected, allowing for enhancements to the zero order *ES*, the power charts in Chapter 4 (or tables in Cohen, 1977, 1988; or Kraemer & Thiemann, 1987) can be consulted to determine the minimal sample size for each experimental group required under the selected alpha and beta levels. At this point, increased power can be attained by employing a sample larger than the minimum indicated in those chapters. If there are limits on the numbers of subjects available or appropriate for one experimental condition, power may be increased by adding more subjects to the other condition (unequal *n*, see Chapter 6).

If the number of subjects available falls below the necessary minimum, the researcher might, as a last resort, consider relaxing alpha from the value initially set. This is less desirable than other approaches to increasing power, however. First, unless alpha is relaxed to rather extreme values it has only modest effects on power. Second, what improvement in power is gained by this tactic comes, by definition, at the expense of increased probability of Type I error—not a very desirable trade-off in many circumstances. Finally, of course, the researcher can relax beta, that is, accept a power level lower than the criterion initially adopted for the power analysis. There may be situations in which it is necessary to relax both alpha and beta to fairly liberal levels—for example, .20—in order to keep power at a defensible level.

While this overview of strategy provides some general guidelines, the key to designing sensitive treatment effectiveness research is to understand the factors that influence statistical power and apply that knowledge adroitly to the planning and implementation of each study undertaken. As an aid to recall and application, the factors discussed in this volume that play a role in the statistical power of experimental research are listed in Table 8.1.

Learning to Live with Power Problems

Attaining adequate statistical power in treatment effectiveness research is not an easy matter. The basic dilemma, as indicated throughout this vol-

TABLE 8.1 Factors That Work to Increase Statistical Power in Treatment Effectiveness Research and the Chapter(s) Where Each Is Discussed

---

Independent variable

Strong treatment, high dosage in the treatment condition (1,2,**7**)
Untreated or low dosage control condition for high contrast with treatment (**7**)
Treatment integrity; uniform application of treatment to recipients (1,2,**7**)
Control group integrity; uniform control conditions for recipients (1,2,**7**)

Subjects

Large sample size in each experimental condition (1,2,4,**6**)
Increased numbers in one condition when fixed sample size in other (**6**)
Deploying limited subjects into few rather than many experimental groups (**6**)
Little initial heterogeneity on dependent variable (1,2,**5**)
Measurement or variance control of subject heterogeneity (1,4,5,**6**)
Uniform response of subjects to treatment (1,6,**7**)
Differential subject response accounted for statistically (interactions) (**6**)

Dependent variables

Validity for measuring characteristic expected to change (1,2,5,**7**)
Validity, sensitivity for change on characteristic measured (1,2,**5**)
Fine-grained units of measurement rather than coarse or categorical (1,2,**5**)
No floor or ceiling effects in the range of expected response (1,2,**5**)
Mastery or criterion-oriented rather than individual differences measures (2,**5**)
Inherent reliability in measure; unresponsiveness to irrelevant factors (1,2,**5**)
Consistency in measurement procedures (1,2,**5**)
Aggregation of unreliable measures (**5**)
Timing of measurement to coincide with peak response to treatment (1,**7**)
Measurement of more proximal effects rather than more distal ones (**7**)

Statistical analysis

Larger alpha for significance testing (2,4,**6**)
One-tailed directional tests rather than two-tailed nondirectional ones (1,2,4,**6**)
Significance tests for graduated scores, not ordinal or categorical (1,2,**5**)
Statistical variance control; blocking, pairing, ANCOVA, interactions (1,2,4,5,**6**)

NOTE: The bold number indicates the chapter with the most extensive discussion of each topic.

ume, is that high power requires either a large effect size or a large sample size or both. Despite their potential practical significance, however, the treatments of interest all too often produce modest statistical effects and the samples upon which they can be studied are often of limited size. The result, as shown in Chapter 1, is a pervasive problem of low statistical power and, correspondingly, high Type II error rates.

Treatment effectiveness research, as a field, needs to learn to live responsibly with this problem. The most important elements of a coping strategy are to recognize the predicament and attempt to overcome it in every way possible when a study is designed. That is what this book is all about. There are other aspects of an appropriate strategy for the field, however, that deserve some mention in these closing pages, namely: (1) alternatives to experimental research, (2) full disclosure in reporting treatment effectiveness research, and (3) meta-analysis.

Alternatives to experimental research. One option that should be seriously considered in treatment effectiveness research is that of not conducting experimental research at all. In many instances, a careful correlational or qualitative study might produce more useful information with the same effort. The strength of experimental research is that it probes the cause and effect relationship between a treatment and its effects. While causality is an important issue in treatment, it is not the only issue. Many aspects of treatment delivery, the nature of the treatment, and the responses and conditions for response by its intended beneficiaries deserve close study and do not always necessitate experimental design.

In addition, as argued throughout this volume, there are various conceptual and methodological preliminaries that warrant research attention before good treatment effectiveness research can be designed. Among these are development of treatment theory, measurement of treatment strength and integrity, investigation of candidate dependent measures, identification of sources of subject heterogeneity and appropriate covariates, and the like. Study of these matters generally requires some mix of descriptive, correlational, and qualitative research that typically raises less acute power issues than does experimental research.

Reporting treatment effectiveness research. Perhaps the most pernicious aspect of the power problem in treatment effectiveness research is that it is so often invisible when research is reported and reviewed. It is imperative, therefore, for researchers to identify explicitly and disclose fully the features of their studies that bear on statistical power. Some form of power analysis, for example, should be routinely described. That description should include, at the least, a statement regarding the minimal effect size considered meaningful and the power of the study for detecting that effect. It is also very useful for other researchers if the specific information most pertinent to power is fully reported: the means and standard deviations on each dependent measure for each experimental group (adjusted and unadjusted if variance control techniques are used), correlations between co-variates and dependent measures, the sample sizes, the strength and integrity of treatment, the timing of measurement, and so forth.

One very specific suggestion can be made regarding the reporting of treatment effectiveness research, especially low powered instances. The results of statistical significance testing should be presented in confidence interval form rather than as a *p*-value and a statement of whether significance was attained (Reichardt & Gollob, 1987). A confidence interval, recall, brackets the range within which the difference between the treatment and control group means can be expected to fall at the confidence level specified by 1-α (Chapter 6). If that bracket includes zero, that is, no difference between means, than the null hypothesis is not rejected and the finding is judged statistically nonsignificant.

More important, however, is the fact that the width of the confidence interval is a direct indicator of the power of the significance test. Low powered research produces very wide intervals, high powered research yields narrow ones. With confidence interval information it is possible to inspect the whole range of mean differences that are consistent with the data from the study. A wide interval, though it may contain zero and thus be consistent with the null hypothesis, may also contain large values and thus be equally consistent with the proposition that the treatment has substantial effects.

The value of confidence interval information is further enhanced if it is presented in effect size terms. That is, rather than a bracket for the range of $\bar{X}_t - \bar{X}_c$, those values can be divided throughout by the appropriate standard deviation and reported as a range of effect sizes. Inclusion of $ES = 0$ in that range still signals the viability of the null hypothesis but inclusion of effects as large as, say, .50 or .75 standard deviations indicates very directly the size of the nonzero effects that are also possible. Confidence intervals in *ES* terms also communicate even more clearly just how much power the study possessed, or how little.

Meta-analysis. In broad perspective, judgment about the effectiveness of a particular treatment approach is rarely made on the basis of a single study. Any one study necessarily has unique features that render the dependability of its conclusions at least somewhat uncertain. A more robust assessment is provided by a number of studies of a treatment, or its variants, especially if they are conducted by different researchers at different sites under different circumstances. Such a collection of studies, of course, must somehow be integrated and interpreted before its collective result can be discerned. That function is typically performed by the research review—an integrative review of the research literature on the effectiveness of the treatment at issue.

One form of integrative research review, meta-analysis, is of particular interest in the context of statistical power (aside from its use in Chapters 1 and 3 of this volume). Meta-analysis approaches the task of integrating treatment effectiveness research by statistically aggregating the research results, literally making a data set out of effect sizes and analyzing them in various ways (Glass et al., 1981; Hedges & Olkin, 1985; Hunter, Schmidt, & Jackson, 1982; Rosenthal, 1984). When multiple studies are combined statistically, the combination, not surprisingly, has more power than any of the single studies taken alone. Meta-analysis, therefore, can be seen as a technique for increasing statistical power—a technique that applies to groups of studies rather than to the individual studies that have been the emphasis of this volume.

The pervasive power problems of treatment effectiveness research make meta-analysis an especially significant tool in that context. In particular, meta-analysis offers an avenue by which low powered studies can make a useful contribution to research on treatment effectiveness. This does not excuse researchers from attempting to design research with adequate power since it is important that each individual study be as meaningful and credible as possible. It does mean, however, that a high quality, small n study can be worth doing so long as the researcher understands and discloses its limitations. A researcher in such a case may be somewhat abashed to recognize that the primary value of his or her study is to be a data point in a meta-analysis, but this accomplishment should nonetheless be recognized as a valuable contribution in its own right.

To realize fully the potential of meta-analysis in treatment effectiveness research, each individual study must report the information, both statistical and nonstatistical, that permits effective meta-analysis (Mosteller, Gilbert, & McPeek, 1980). While this is not the place for a detailed specification of appropriate reporting standards, it should be noted that much of the information needed for meta-analysis is the same as that pertinent to statistical power—effect sizes, sample sizes, strength and integrity of treatment, subject characteristics, and the like.

A Concluding Editorial

Formulated as experimental design, treatment effectiveness research is the bedrock for basic research in the behavioral sciences. Applied to promising practical interventions in education, health, mental health, social services, criminal justice, and a host of other such domains, it is one of our most probing and cogent tools for identifying the means by which people problems can be ameliorated and our collective quality of life improved. Treatment effectiveness research is too important for us to fail to do it as well as we possibly can. The widespread neglect of statistical power and the parade of uninterpretable null results that follows from that neglect, especially in applied research, should be an embarrassment to the behavioral sciences. The remedy is to make better application of what we already know about power, work vigorously to expand that knowledge, and report honestly and clearly the limitations of our efforts for each study we undertake. It is my hope that this volume will support and encourage those salutary developments.

Reference Appendix for Meta-Analyses
Cited in Table 3.3

1. Administration for Children, Youth, and Families (1983). *The effects of the Head Start program on children's cognitive development.* Preliminary report, Head Start evaluation, synthesis, and utilization project. Washington, DC: DHHS. (ERIC #ED 248 989).
2. Aiello, N. C. (1981). *A meta-analysis comparing alternative methods of individualized and traditional instruction in science.* Unpublished doctoral dissertation, Virginia Polytechnic Institute and State University.
3. Aiello, N. C., & Wolfle, L. M. (1980). *A meta-analysis of individualized instruction in science.* (ERIC #ED 190 404)
4. Almeida, M. C., & Denham, S. A. (1984). *Interpersonal cognitive problem-solving: A meta-analysis.* (ERIC #ED 247 003)
5. Andrews, G., Guitar, B., & Howie, P. (1980). Meta-analysis of the effects of stuttering treatment. *Journal of Speech and Hearing Disorders, 45,* 287–307.
6. Andrews, G., & Harvey, R. (1981). Does psychotherapy benefit neurotic patients? A reanalysis of the Smith, Glass, and Miller data. *Archives of General Psychiatry, 38,* 1203–1208.
7. Angert, J. F., & Clark, F. E. (1982). *Finding the rose among the thorns: Some thoughts on integrating media research.* Association for Educational Communications and Technology. (ERIC #ED 223 192)
8. Asencio, C. E. (1984). *Effects of behavioral objectives on student achievement: A meta analysis of findings.* Doctoral dissertation, Florida State University. (UMI #84-12499)
9. Athappilly, K., Smidchens, U., & Kofel, J. W. (1983). A computer-based meta-analysis of the effects of modern mathematics in comparison with traditional mathematics. *Educational Evaluation and Policy Analysis, 5,* 485–493.
10. Baker, S. B., & Popowicz, C. L. (1983). Meta-analysis as a strategy for evaluating effects of career education interventions. *The Vocational Guidance Quarterly, 31,* 178–186.
11. Baker, S. B., Swisher, J. D., Nadenichek, P. E., & Popowicz, C. L. (1984). Measured effects of primary prevention strategies. *Personnel and Guidance Journal, 62,* 459–464.
12. Bangert, R. L., Kulik, J. A., & Kulik, C. C. (1983). Individualized systems of instruction in secondary schools. *Review of Educational Research, 53,* 143–158.

NOTE: ERIC = Educational Resources Information Center
UMI = University Microfilms International

13. Bangert, R. L., Kulik, J. A., & Kulik, C. C. (1983). Effects of coaching programs on achievement test performance. *Review of Educational Research, 53*, 571–585.
14. Bangert-Drowns, R. L., Kulik, J. A., & Kulik, C. C. (1985). Effectiveness of computer-based education in secondary schools. *Journal of Computer-Based Instruction, 12*, 59–68.
15. Berman, J. S., Miller, R. C., & Massman, P. J. (1985). Cognitive therapy versus systematic desensitization: Is one treatment superior? *Psychological Bulletin, 97*, 451–461.
16. Blanchard, E. B., Andrasik, F., Ahles, T. I., Teders, S. J., & O'Keefe, D. (1980). Migraine and tension headache: A meta-analytic review. *Behavior Therapy, 11*, 613–631.
17. Boulanger, F. D. (1981). Instruction and science learning: A quantitative synthesis. *Journal of Research in Science Teaching, 18*, 311–327.
18. Branwen, M. F. (1982). *Meta-analysis of the effectiveness of assertion training groups.* Doctoral dissertation, University of Wisconsin-Madison. (UMI #82-15931)
19. Bredderman, T. (1983). Effects of activity-based elementary science on student outcomes: A quantitative synthesis. *Review of Educational Research, 53*, 499–518.
20. Burke, M. J., & Day, R. R. (1986). A cumulative study of the effectiveness of managerial training. *Journal of Applied Psychology, 71*, 232–245.
21. Burns, P. K. (1981). *A quantitative synthesis of research findings relative to the pedagogical effectiveness of computer-assisted mathematics instruction in elementary and secondary schools.* Unpublished doctoral dissertation, The University of Iowa.
22. Carlberg, C., & Kavale, K. (1980). The efficacy of special versus regular class placement for exceptional children: A meta-analysis. *Journal of Special Education, 14*, 295–309.
23. Carlson, M. (1987). *Social and academic outcomes of cooperative learning in the mainstreamed classroom: A meta-analysis.* Unpublished manuscript, Claremont Graduate School, Claremont, California.
24. Casey, R. J., & Berman, J. S. (1985). The outcome of psychotherapy with children. *Psychological Bulletin, 98*, 388–400.
25. Casto, G., & Mastropieri, M. A. (1986). The efficacy of early intervention programs: A meta-analysis. *Exceptional Children, 52*, 417–424.
26. Casto, G., & White, K. (1984). The efficacy of early intervention programs with environmentally at-risk infants. *Journal of Children in Contemporary Society, 17*, 37–50.
27. Cedar, R. B. (1985). *A meta-analysis of the parent effectiveness training outcome research literature.* Doctoral dissertation, Boston University. (UMI #86-09263)
28. Champney, T. F., & Schulz, E. M. (1983). *A reassessment of the effects of psychotherapy.* Midwestern Psychological Association. (ERIC #ED 237 895)
29. Cohen, P. A. (1980). Effectiveness of student-rating feedback for improving college instruction: A meta-analysis of findings. *Research in Higher Education, 13*, 321–341.
30. Cohen, P. A., Ebeling, B. J., & Kulik, J. A. (1981). A meta-analysis of outcome studies of visual-based instruction. *Educational Communication and Technology, 29*, 26–36.
31. Cohen, P. A., Kulik, J. A., & Kulik, C. C. (1982). Educational outcomes of tutoring: A meta-analysis of findings. *American Educational Research Journal, 19*, 237–248.
32. Cohn, C. M. G. (1984). *Creativity training effectiveness: A research synthesis.* Doctoral dissertation, Arizona State University. (UMI #84-24639)
33. Cohn, C. L. (1985). A meta-analysis of the effects of teaching innovations on achieve-

ment in college economics. Doctoral dissertation, Illinois State University. (UMI #86-08948)

34. Collins, R. C. (1984). *Head Start: A review of research with implications for practice in early childhood education.* American Educational Research Association. (ERIC #ED 245 833)

35. Colosimo, M. L. (1981). *The effect of practice or beginning teaching on the self concepts and attitudes of teachers: A quantitative synthesis.* Unpublished doctoral dissertation, University of Chicago.

36. Colosimo, M. L. (1984). Attitude change with initial teaching experience. *College Student Journal, 18,* 119–125.

37. Cook, S. B., Scruggs, T. E., Mastropieri, M. A., & Casto, G. C. (1986). Handicapped students as tutors. *Journal of Special Education, 19,* 483–492.

38. Curbelo, J. (1984). *Effects of problem-solving instruction on science and mathematics student achievement: A meta-analysis of findings.* Doctoral dissertation, Florida State University. (UMI #85-05290)

39. Dekkers, J., & Donatti, S. (1981). The integration of research studies on the use of simulation as an instructional strategy. *Journal of Educational Research, 74,* 424–427.

40. Denham, S. A., & Almeida, M. C. (1987). Children's social problem-solving skills, behavioral adjustment, and interventions: A meta-analysis evaluating theory and practice. *Journal of Applied Developmental Psychology, 8,* 391–409.

41. DerSimonian, R., & Laird, N. M. (1983). Evaluating the effect of coaching on SAT scores: A meta-analysis. *Harvard Educational Review, 53,* 1–15.

42. Devine, E. C. (1983). *Effects of psychoeducational interventions: A meta-analytic review of studies with surgical patients.* Doctoral dissertation, University of Illinois at Chicago. (UMI #84-04400)

43. Devine, E. C., & Cook, T. D. (1983). A meta-analytic analysis of effects of psychoeducational interventions on length of postsurgical hospital stay. *Nursing Research, 32,* 267–274.

44. Dole, A. A., Rockey, P. B., & DiTomasso, R. (1983). *Meta-analysis of outcome research in reducing test anxiety: Interventions, rigor, and inertia.* American Educational Research Association. (ERIC #ED 231 844)

45. Dush, D. M., Hirt, M. L., & Schroeder, H. (1983). Self-statement modification with adults: A meta-analysis. *Psychological Bulletin, 94,* 408–422.

46. El-Nemr, M. A. (1979). *A meta-analysis of the outcomes of teaching biology as inquiry.* Doctoral dissertation, University of Colorado. (UMI #80-11274)

47. Enz, J., Horak, & Blecha (1982). *Review and analysis of reports of science inservice projects: Recommendations for the future.* National Science Teachers Association. (ERIC #ED 216 883)

48. Eppley, K., Abrams, A., & Shear, J. (undated). *The effects of meditation and relaxation techniques: A meta-analysis.* Unpublished manuscript, Lawrence Livermore National Laboratory, Livermore, California.

49. Falcone, A. J. (1985). *Meta-analysis of personnel training techniques for three populations.* Doctoral dissertation, Illinois Institute of Technology. (UMI #86-06497)

50. Feehan, G. G. (1984). *A meta-analysis of psychotherapeutic interventions for the cessation and reduction of smoking.* Unpublished doctoral dissertation, University of Manitoba.

51. Feltz, D. L., & Landers, D. M. (1983). The effects of mental practice on motor skill learning and performance: A meta-analysis. *Journal of Sport Psychology, 5,* 25–57.

180   DESIGN SENSITIVITY

52. Ferguson, P. C. (1981). *An integrative meta-analysis of psychological studies investigating the treatment outcomes of meditation techniques.* Doctoral dissertation, University of Colorado. (UMI #81-22282)
53. Fuchs, D., & Fuchs, L. S. (1985). *The importance of context in testing: A meta-analysis.* American Educational Research Association. (ERIC #ED 255 559)
54. Fuchs, L. S., & Fuchs, D. (1986). Effects of systematic formative evaluation: A meta-analysis. *Exceptional Children, 53,* 199–208.
55. Garrett, C. J. (1984). *Meta-analysis of the effects of institutional and community residential treatment on adjudicated delinquents.* Doctoral dissertation, University of Colorado. (UMI #84-22608)
56. Garrett, C. J. (1985). Effects of residential treatment on adjudicated delinquents: A meta-analysis. *Journal of Research in Crime and Delinquency, 22,* 287–308.
57. Giaconia, R. M. & Hedges, L. V. (1982). Identifying features of effective open education. *Review of Educational Research, 52,* 579–602.
58. Giblin, P., Sprenkle, D. H., & Sheehan, R. (1985). Enrichment outcome research: A meta-analysis of premarital, marital, and family interventions. *Journal of Marital and Family Therapy, 11,* 257–271.
59. Glass, G. V., & Smith, M. L. (1979). Meta-analysis of research on class size and achievement. *Educational Evaluation and Policy Analysis, 1,* 2–16.
60. Goldring, E. B., & Presbrey, L. S. (1986). Evaluating preschool programs: A meta-analytic approach. *Educational Evaluation and Policy Analysis, 8,* 179–188.
61. Gottschalk, R., Davidson, W. S., Gensheimer, L. K., & Mayer, J. P. (1987). Community-based interventions. In H. C. Quay (Ed.), *Handbook of juvenile delinquency.* New York. John Wiley.
62. Graue, M. E., Weinstein, T., & Walberg, H. J. (1983). School-based home instruction and learning: A quantitative synthesis. *Journal of Educational Research, 76,* 351–360.
63. Guskey, T. R., & Gates, S. L. (1985). *A synthesis of research on group-based mastery learning programs.* American Educational Research Association. (ERIC #ED 262 088)
64. Guzzo, R. A., Jette, R. D., & Katzell, R. A. (1985). The effects of psychologically based intervention programs on worker productivity: A meta-analysis. *Personnel Psychology, 38,* 275–291.
65. Harrison, D. (1980). *Meta-analysis of selected studies of staff development.* Doctoral dissertation, University of Florida. (UMI #81-05580)
66. Hartley, S. S. (1977). *Meta-analysis of the effects of individually paced instruction in mathematics.* Doctoral dissertation, University of Colorado. (UMI #77-29926)
67. Hathaway, D. K. (1984). Meta-analysis of studies which examine the effect preoperative instruction of adults has on postoperative outcomes. Doctoral dissertation, University of Texas, Austin. (UMI #85-08277)
68. Hazelrigg, M. D., Cooper, H. M., & Borduin, C. M. (1987). Evaluating the effectiveness of family therapies: An integrative review and analysis. *Psychological Bulletin, 101,* 428–442.
69. Hedges, L. V., & Stock, W. (1983). The effects of class size: An examination of rival hypotheses. *American Educational Research Journal, 20,* 63–85.
70. Hembree, R. (1984). *Model for meta-analysis of research in education with a demonstration in mathematics education: Effects of hand held calculators.* Doctoral dissertation, University of Tennessee. (UMI #84-29597)
71. Henk, W. A., & Stahl, N. A. (1985). *A meta-analysis of the effect of notetaking on learning from lecture.* National Reading Conference. (ERIC #ED 258 533)
72. Hetzel, D. C., Rasher, Butcher, & Walberg (1980). *A quantitative synthesis of the ef-*

fects of open education. American Educational Research Association. (ERIC #ED 191 902)

73. Hillocks, G. (1984). What works in teaching composition: A meta-analysis of experimental treatment studies. *American Journal of Education, 93*, 133–170.

74. Horak, V. M. (1981). A meta-analysis of research findings on individualized instruction in mathematics. *Journal of Educational Research, 74*, 249–253.

75. Horak, W. J. (1985). *A meta-analysis of learning science concepts from textual materials*. National Association for Research in Science Teaching. (ERIC #ED 256 629)

76. Horon, P. F., & Lynn, D. D. (1980). Learning hierarchies research. *Evaluation in Education, 4*, 82–83.

77. Howell, J. K. (1984). *Effects of preoperative preparation of children having minor surgery: A literary synthesis with meta-analysis*. Doctoral dissertation, University of Texas, Austin. (UMI #85-13231)

78. Iverson, B. K., & Levy, S. R. (1982). Using meta-analysis in health education research. *The Journal of School Health, 52*, 234–239.

79. Johnson, D. W., Johnson, R. T., & Maruyama, G. (1983). Interdependence and interpersonal attraction among heterogeneous and homogeneous individuals: A theoretical formulation and a meta-analysis of the research. *Review of Educational Research, 53*, 5–54.

80. Johnson, D. W., Maruyama, G., Johnson, R., Nelson, D., & Skon, L. (1981). Effects of cooperative, competitive, and individualistic goal structures on achievement: A meta-analysis. *Psychological Bulletin, 89*, 47–62.

81. Jones, L. C. (1983). *A meta-analytic study of the effects of childbirth education research from 1960 to 1981*. Doctoral dissertation, Texas A & M University. (UMI #83-23680)

82. Joslin, P. A. (1980). *Inservice teacher education: A meta-analysis of the research*. Doctoral dissertation, University of Minnesota. (UMI #81-02055)

83. Kaufman, P. (1985). *Meta-analysis of juvenile delinquency prevention programs*. Unpublished masters thesis, Claremont Graduate School, Claremont, California.

84. Kavale, K. (1980). Psycholinguistic training. *Evaluation in Education, 4*, 88–90.

85. Kavale, K. (1981). Functions of the Illinois Test of Psycholinguistic Abilities (ITPA): Are they trainable? *Exceptional Children, 47*, 496–510.

86. Kavale, K. (1982). Psycholinguistic training programs: Are there differential treatment effects? *Exceptional Child, 29*, 21–30.

87. Kavale, K. A. (1984). A meta-analytic evaluation of the Frostig test and training program. *Exceptional Child, 31*, 134–141.

88. Kavale, K. A., & Forness, S. R. (1983). Hyperactivity and diet treatment: A meta-analysis of the Feingold hypothesis. *Journal of Learning Disabilities, 16*, 324–330.

89. Kavale, K., & Mattson, P. D. (1983). One jumped off the balance beam: Meta-analysis of perceptual-motor training. *Journal of Learning Disabilities, 16*, 165–173.

90. Klauer, K. J. (1984). Intentional and incidental learning with instructional texts: A meta-analysis for 1970–1980. *American Educational Research Journal, 21*, 323–339.

91. Kozlow, M. J. (1978). *A meta-analysis of selected advance organizer research reports from 1960–1977*. Doctoral dissertation, Ohio State University. (ERIC #ED 161 755)

92. Kozlow, M. J., & White, A. L. (1980). Advance organizer research. *Evaluation in Education, 4*, 47–48.

93. Kulik, J. A., Bangert, R. L., & Williams, G. W. (1983). Effects of computer-based teaching on secondary school students. *Journal of Educational Psychology, 75*, 19–26.

94. Kulik, J. A., Bangert-Drowns, R. L., & Kulik, C. C. (1984). Effectiveness of coaching for aptitude tests. *Psychological Bulletin, 95,* 179–188.
95. Kulik, J. A., Cohen, P. A., & Ebeling, B. J. (1980). Effectiveness of programmed instruction in higher education: A meta-analysis of findings. *Educational Evaluation and Policy Analysis, 2,* 51–63.
96. Kulik, C. C., & Kulik, J. A. (1982). Effects of ability grouping on secondary school students: A meta-analysis of evaluation findings. *American Educational Research Journal, 19,* 415–428.
97. Kulik, C. C., & Kulik, J. A. (1982). Research synthesis on ability grouping. *Educational Leadership, 29,* 619–621.
98. Kulik, C. C., & Kulik, J. A. (1984). *Effects of ability grouping on elementary school pupils: A meta-analysis.* American Psychological Association. (ERIC #ED 255 329)
99. Kulik, J. A., & Kulik, C. C. (1984). Effects of accelerated instruction on students. *Review of Educational Research, 54,* 409–425.
100. Kulik, J. A., Kulik, C. C., & Bangert, R. L. (1984). Effects of practice on aptitude and achievement test scores. *American Educational Research Journal, 21,* 435–447.
101. Kulik, C. C., Kulik, J. A., & Bangert-Drowns, R. L. (1984). *Effects of computer-based education on elementary school pupils.* American Educational Research Association. (ERIC #ED 244 616)
102. Kulik, J. A., Kulik, C. C., & Cohen, P. A. (1979). A meta-analysis of outcome studies of Keller's personalized system of instruction. *American Psychologist, 34,* 307–318.
103. Kulik, J. A., Kulik, C. C., & Cohen, P. A. (1979). Research on audio-tutorial instruction: A meta-analysis of comparative studies. *Research in Higher Education, 11,* 321–341.
104. Kulik, C. C., Kulik, J. A., & Cohen, P. A. (1980). Effectiveness of computer-based college teaching: A meta-analysis of findings. *Review of Educational Research, 50,* 525–544.
105. Kulik, C. C., Kulik, J. A., & Schwalb, B. J. (1983). College programs for high-risk and disadvantaged students: A meta-analysis of findings. *Review of Educational Research, 53,* 397–414.
106. Kulik, C. C., Schwalb, B. J., & Kulik, J. A. (1982). Programmed instruction in secondary education: A meta-analysis of evaluation findings. *Journal of Educational Research, 75,* 133–138.
107. Kyle, W. C. (1982). *A meta-analysis of the effects on student performance of new curricular programs developed in science education since 1955.* Doctoral dissertation, University of Iowa. (UMI #82-22249)
108. Landman, J. T., & Dawes, R. M. (1982). Psychotherapy outcome: Smith and Glass' conclusions stand up under scrutiny. *American Psychologist, 37,* 504–516.
109. Levy, S. R., Iverson, B. K., & Walberg, H. J. (1980). Nutrition-education research: An interdisciplinary evaluation and review. *Health Education Quarterly, 7,* 107–126.
110. Lott, G. W. (1983). The effect of inquiry teaching and advance organizers upon student outcomes in science education. *Journal of Research in Science Teaching, 20,* 437–451.
111. Luiten, J. W. (1980). Advance organizers in learning. *Evaluation in Education, 4,* 49–50.
112. Luiten, J., Ames, W., & Ackerson, G. (1980). A meta-analysis of the effects of advance organizers on learning and retention. *American Educational Research Journal, 17,* 211–218.

113. Lyday, N. L. (1983). *A meta-analysis of the adjunct question literature.* Doctoral dissertation, Pennsylvania State University. (UMI #84-09065)
114. Lysakowski, R. S., & Walberg, H. J. (1980). Classroom reinforcement. *Evaluation in Education, 4,* 115–116.
115. Lysakowski, R. S., & Walberg, H. J. (1981). Classroom reinforcement and learning: A quantitative synthesis. *Journal of Educational Research, 75,* 69–77.
116. Lysakowski, R. S., & Walberg, H. J. (1982). Instructional effects of cues, participation, and corrective feedback: A quantitative synthesis. *American Educational Research Journal, 19,* 559–578.
117. Madamba, S. R. (1980). *Meta-analysis on the effects of open and traditional schooling on the teaching-learning of reading.* Doctoral dissertation, University of California, Los Angeles. (UMI #81-02856)
118. Malone, M. R. (1984). *Project MAFEX: Report on preservice field experiences in science education.* National Association for Research in Science Teaching. (ERIC #ED 244 928)
119. Marcucci, R. G. (1980). *A meta-analysis of research on methods of teaching mathematical problem-solving.* Doctoral dissertation, University of Iowa. (UMI #80-28278)
120. Mattson, P. D. (1985). *A meta-analysis of learning and memory in mental retardation.* Doctoral dissertation, University of California, Riverside. (UMI #85-20636)
121. Mazzuca, S. A. (1982). Does patient education in chronic disease have therapeutic value? *Journal of Chronic Disease, 35,* 521–529.
122. McEvoy, G. M., & Cascio, W. F. (1985). Strategies for reducing employee turnover: A meta-analysis. *Journal of Applied Psychology, 70,* 342–353.
123. Messick, S., & Jungeblut, A. (1981). Time and method in coaching for the SAT. *Psychological Bulletin, 89,* 191–216.
124. Miller, R. C., & Berman, J. S. (1983). The efficacy of cognitive behavior therapies: A quantitative review of the research evidence. *Psychological Bulletin, 94,* 39–53.
125. Moore, D. W., & Readence, J. E. (1984). A quantitative and qualitative review of graphic organizer research. *Journal of Educational Research, 78,* 11–17.
126. Mumford, E., Schlesinger, H. J., & Glass, G. V. (1982). The effects of psychological intervention on recovery from surgery and heart attacks: An analysis of the literature. *American Journal of Public Health, 72,* 141–151.
127. Nicholson, R. A., & Berman, J. S. (1983). Is follow-up necessary in evaluating psychotherapy? *Psychological Bulletin, 93,* 261–278.
128. Niemiec, R. P. (1984). *The meta-analysis of computer assisted instruction at the elementary school level.* Doctoral dissertation, University of Illinois at Chicago. (UMI #85-01250)
129. Noland, T. K. (1985). *The effects of ability grouping: A meta-analysis of research findings.* Doctoral dissertation, University of Colorado. (UMI #85-28511)
130. Nye, C., Foster, S. H., & Seaman, D. (1987). Effectiveness of language intervention with the language/learning disabled. *Journal of Speech and Hearing Disorders, 52,* 348–357.
131. O'Bryan, V. L. (1985). *The treatment of test anxiety: A meta-analytic review.* Doctoral dissertation, Ohio University. (UMI #85-23654)
132. O'Flynn, A. I. (1982). *Meta-analysis of behavioral intervention effects on weight loss in the obese.* Doctoral dissertation, University of Connecticut. (UMI #83-02083)
133. Ottenbacher, K. (1982). Sensory integration therapy: Affect or effect. *American Journal of Occupational Therapy, 36,* 571–578.

134. Ottenbacher, K. J., & Petersen, P. (1984). The efficacy of vestibular stimulation as a form of specific sensory enrichment. *Clinical Pediatrics, 23,* 428–433.
135. Ottenbacher, K., & Petersen, P. (1985). The efficacy of early intervention programs for children with organic impairment: A quantitative review. *Evaluation and Program Planning, 8,* 135–146.
136. Parham, J. L. (1983). *A meta-analysis of the use of manipulative materials and student achievement in elementary school mathematics.* Doctoral dissertation, Auburn University. (UMI #83-12477)
137. Paschal, R. A., Weinstein, T., & Walberg, H. J. (1984). The effects of homework on learning: A quantitative synthesis. *Journal of Educational Research, 78,* 97–104.
138. Peterson, P. L. (1980). Open versus traditional classrooms. *Evaluation in Education, 4,* 58–60.
139. Pflaum, S. W., Walberg, H. J., Karegianes, M. L., & Rasher, S. P. (1980). Reading instruction: A quantitative synthesis. *Educational Researcher, 9,* 12–18.
140. Phillips, G. W. (1983). *Learning the conservation concept: A meta-analysis.* Doctoral dissertation, University of Kentucky. (UMI #83-22983)
141. Polder, S. K. (1986). *A meta-analysis of cognitive behavior therapy.* Unpublished doctoral dissertation, University of Wisconsin-Madison.
142. Posavac, E. J. (1980). Evaluations of patient education programs: A meta-analysis. *Evaluation and the Health Professions, 3,* 47–62.
143. Posavac, E. J., Sinacore, J. M., Brotherton, S. E., Helford, M. C., & Turpin, R. S. (1985). Increasing compliance to medical treatment regimens: A meta-analysis of program evaluation. *Evaluation and the Health Professions, 8,* 7–22.
144. Powell, G. (1980). *A meta-analysis of the effects of 'imposed' and 'induced' imagery upon word recall.* National Reading Conference. (ERIC #ED 199 644)
145. Prince Henry Hospital (1983). A treatment outline for depressive disorders: The quality assurance project. *Australian and New Zealand Journal of Psychiatry, 17,* 129–146.
146. Prioleau, L., Murdock, M., & Brody, N. (1983). An analysis of psychotherapy versus placebo studies. *The Behavioral and Brain Sciences, 6,* 275–310.
147. Readence, J., & Moore, D. W. (1981). A meta-analytic review of the effect of adjunct pictures on reading comprehension. *Psychology in the Schools, 18,* 218–224.
148. Redfield, D. L., & Rousseau, E. W. (1981). A meta-analysis of experimental research on teacher questioning behavior. *Review of Educational Research, 51,* 237–245.
149. Reilly, R. R., Brown, B., Blood, M. R., & Malatesta, C. Z. (1981). The effects of realistic previews: A study and discussion of the literature. *Personnel Psychology, 34,* 823–834.
150. Robinson, A. W., & Hyman, I. A. (1984). *A meta-analysis of human relations teacher training programs.* National Association of School Psychologists. (ERIC #ED 253 521)
151. Rock, S. L. (1985). *A meta-analysis of self-instructional training research.* Doctoral dissertation, University of Illinois. (UMI #86-00295)
152. Rose, L. H., & Lin, H. T. (1984). A meta-analysis of long-term creativity training programs. *Journal of Creative Behavior, 18,* 11–22.
153. Rosenbaum, C. M. (1983). *A meta-analysis of the effectiveness of educational treatment programs for emotionally disturbed students.* Doctoral dissertation, College of William and Mary. (UMI #83-17068)
154. Samson, G. E. (1985). Effects of training in test-taking skills on achievement test performance: A quantitative synthesis. *Journal of Educational Research, 78,* 261–266.

155. Samson, G. E., Borger, J. B., Weinstein, T., & Walberg, H. J. (1984). Pre-teaching experiences and attitudes: A quantitative synthesis. *Journal of Research and Development in Education, 17,* 52–56.
156. Sanders, V. H. (1979). *A meta-analysis: The relationship of program content and operation factors to measured effectiveness of college reading-study programs.* Doctoral dissertation, University of the Pacific. (UMI #79–23975)
157. Schermer, J. D. (1983). *Visual media and attitude formation and attitude change in nursing education.* Doctoral dissertation, Wayne State University. (UMI #84-06022)
158. Schimmel, B. J. (1983). *A meta-analysis of feedback to learners in computerized and programmed instruction.* American Educational Research Association. (ERIC #ED 233 708)
159. Schlaefli, A., Rest, J. R., & Thoma, S. J. (1985). Does moral education improve moral judgment? A meta-analysis of intervention studies using the defining issues test. *Review of Educational Research, 55,* 319–352.
160. Schmidt, M., Weinstein, T., Niemiec, R., & Walberg, H. J. (1986). Computer-assisted instruction with exceptional children. *Journal of Special Education, 19,* 493–502.
161. Scruggs, T. E., Bennion, K., & White, K. (1984). Teaching test-taking skills to elementary grade students: A meta-analysis. In Scruggs, T. E., *The administration and interpretation of standardized achievement tests with learning disabled and behaviorally disordered elementary school children.* Final Report, Developmental Center for the Handicapped, Utah University, Salt Lake City. (ERIC #ED 256 082)
162. Shapiro, D. A., & Shapiro, D. (1982). Meta-analysis of comparative therapy outcome studies: A replication and refinement. *Psychological Bulletin, 92,* 581–604.
163. Shapiro, D. A., & Shapiro, D. (1983). Comparative therapy outcome research: Methodological implications of meta-analysis. *Journal of Consulting and Clinical Psychology, 51,* 42–53.
164. Shatz, M. A. (1983). *Assertiveness training: A meta-analysis of the research findings.* Doctoral dissertation, University of Florida. (UMI #83-25006)
165. Shymansky, J. (1984). BSCS programs: Just how effective were they? *American Biology Teacher, 46,* 54–57.
166. Shymansky, J. A., Kyle, W. C., & Alport, J. (1982). Research synthesis on the science curriculum projects of the sixties. *Educational Leadership, 40,* 63–66.
167. Shymansky, J. A., Kyle, W. C., & Alport, J. M. (1983). The effects of new science curricula on student performance. *Journal of Research in Science Teaching, 20,* 387–404.
168. Skiba, R., & Casey, A. (1985). Interventions for behaviorally disordered students: A quantitative review and methodological critique. *Behavioral Disorders, 10,* 239–252.
169. Slavin, R. E. (1987). Ability grouping and student achievement in elementary schools: A best evidence synthesis. *Review of Educational Research, 57,* 293–336.
170. Smith, M. L., & Glass, G. V. (1980). Meta-analysis of research on class size and its relationship to attitudes and instruction. *American Educational Research Journal, 17,* 419–433.
171. Smith, M. L., Glass, G. V., & Miller, T. I. (1980). *The benefits of psychotherapy.* Baltimore: Johns Hopkins University Press.
172. Snyder, S., & Sheehan, R. (1983). Integrating research in early childhood special education: The use of meta-analysis. *Diagnostique, 9,* 12–25.
173. Sprinthall, N. A. (1981). A new model for research in the service of guidance and counseling. *Personnel and Guidance Journal, 59,* 487–494.

174. Stahl, S. A., & Fairbanks, M. M. (1986). The effects of vocabulary instruction: A model-based meta-analysis. *Review of Educational Research, 56,* 72–110.
175. Stein, D. M., & Polyson, J. (1984). The Primary Mental Health Project reconsidered. *Journal of Consulting and Clinical Psychology, 52,* 940–945.
176. Steinbrueck, S. M., Maxwell, S. E., & Howard, G. S. (1983). A meta-analysis of psychotherapy and drug therapy in the treatment of unipolar depression with adults. *Journal of Consulting and Clinical Psychology, 51,* 856–863.
177. Stone, C. L. (1983). A meta-analysis of advance organizer studies. *Journal of Experimental Education, 51,* 194–199.
178. Straw, R. B. (1982). *Meta-analysis of deinstitutionalization in mental health.* Doctoral dissertation, Northwestern University. (UMI #82-26026)
179. Susskind, E. C., & Bond, R. N. (1981). *The potency of primary prevention: A meta-analysis of effect size.* Eastern Psychological Association. (ERIC #ED 214 067)
180. Sweitzer, G. L., & Anderson, R. D. (1983). A meta-analysis of research on science teacher education practices associated with inquiry strategy. *Journal of Research in Science Teaching, 20,* 453–466.
181. Szczurek, M. (1982). *Meta-analysis of simulation games effectiveness for cognitive learning.* Doctoral dissertation, Indiana University. (UMI #82-20735)
182. Tobler, N. S. (1986). Meta-analysis of 143 adolescent drug prevention programs: Quantitative outcome results of program participants compared to a control or comparison group. *Journal of Drug Issues, 16,* 537–567.
183. Truax, M. E. (1983). *A meta-analytic review of studies evaluating paraprofessional effectiveness in mental health, education, law, and social work.* Doctoral dissertation, University of Kansas. (UMI #84-03625)
184. Turley, M. A. (1983). *A meta-analysis of informing mothers concerning the sensory and perceptual capabilities of their infants.* Doctoral dissertation, University of Texas, Austin. (UMI #84-14461)
185. Utah State University Exceptional Child Center (1983). *Early intervention research institute: Final report, 1982–83 work scope.* Utah State University, Logan. (ERIC #ED 250 845)
186. Wade, R. K. (1984). *What makes a difference in inservice teacher education: A meta-analysis of the research.* Doctoral dissertation, University of Massachusetts. (UMI #84-10341)
187. Wade, R. K. (1985). What makes a difference in inservice teacher education? A meta-analysis of research. *Educational Leadership, 42,* 48–54.
188. Wampler, K. S. (1982). Bringing the review of literature into the age of quantification: Meta-analysis as a strategy for integrating research findings in family studies. *Journal of Marriage and the Family, 44,* 1009–1023.
189. Wang, M. C., & Baker, E. T. (1986). Mainstreaming programs: Design features and effects. *Journal of Special Education, 19,* 503–523.
190. Weinstein, T., Boulanger, F. D., & Walberg, H. J. (1982). Science curriculum effects in high school: A quantitative synthesis. *Journal of Research in Science Teaching, 19,* 511–522.
191. Weisz, J. R., Weiss, B., Alicke, M. D., & Klotz, M. L. (1987). Effectiveness of psychotherapy with children and adolescents: A meta-analysis for clinicians. *Journal of Consulting and Clinical Psychology, 55,* 542–549.
192. Willett, J. B., Yamashita, J. M., & Anderson, R. D. (1983). A meta-analysis of instructional systems applied in science teaching. *Journal of Research in Science Teaching, 20,* 405–417.

193. Willig, A. C. (1985). A meta-analysis of selected studies on the effectiveness of bilingual education. *Review of Educational Research, 55,* 269–317.
194. Wilson, L. B., Simson, S., & McCaughey, K. (1983). The status of preventive care for the aged: A meta-analysis. *Prevention in Human Services, 3,* 23–38.
195. Wise, K. C., & Okey, J. R. (1983). A meta-analysis of the effects of various science teaching strategies on achievement. *Journal of Research in Science Teaching, 20,* 419–435.
196. Yeany, R. H., & Miller, P. A. (1983). Effects of diagnostic/remedial instruction on science learning: A meta-analysis. *Journal of Research in Science Teaching, 20,* 19–26.
197. Yeany, R. H., & Porter, C. F. (1982). *The effects of strategy analysis on science teacher behaviors: A meta-analysis.* National Association for Research in Science Teaching. (ERIC #ED 216 858)

References

Abelson, R. P. (1985). A variance explanation paradox: When a little is a lot. *Psychological Bulletin, 97*, 129–133.

Berk, R. A. (Ed.). (1980). *Criterion-referenced measurement: The state of the art.* Baltimore: Johns Hopkins University Press.

Bickman, L. (1987). The functions of program theory. *New Directions for Program Evaluation, 33*, 5–18.

Bonett, D. G. (1982). On post-hoc blocking. *Educational and Psychological Measurement, 42*, 35–39.

Boruch, R. F., & Gomez, H. (1977). Sensitivity, bias, and theory in impact evaluations. *Professional Psychology, 8*, 411–434.

Brennan, R. L. (1980). Applications of generalizability theory. In R. A. Berk (Ed.), *Criterion-referenced measurement: The state of the art* (pp. 186–233). Baltimore: Johns Hopkins University Press.

Brewer, J. K. (1972). On the power of statistical tests in the American Educational Research Journal. *American Educational Research Journal, 9*, 391–401.

Brown, G. W. (1983). Errors, Type I and II. *American Journal of Disorders in Childhood, 137*, 586–591.

Campbell, D. T., & Stanley, J. C. (1966). *Experimental and quasi-experimental designs for research.* Chicago: Rand McNally.

Carver, R. P. (1974). Two dimensions of tests: Psychometric and edumetric. *American Psychologist, 29*, 512–518.

Carver, R. P. (1975). The Coleman Report: Using inappropriately designed achievement tests. *American Educational Research Journal, 12*, 77–86.

Cascio, W. F., Valenzi, E. R., & Silbey, V. A. (1980). More on validation and statistical power. *Journal of Applied Psychology, 65*, 135–138.

Cascio, W. F., & Zedeck, S. (1983). Open a new window in rational research planning: Adjust alpha to maximize statistical power. *Personnel Psychology, 36*, 517–526.

Chase, L. J., & Baran, S. J. (1976). An assessment of quantitative research in mass communication. *Journalism Quarterly, 53*, 308–311.

Chase, L. J., & Chase, R. B. (1976). A statistical power analysis of applied psychological research. *Journal of Applied Psychology, 61*, 234–237.

Chase, L. J., & Tucker, R. K. (1975). A power-analytic examination of contemporary communication research. *Speech Monographs, 42*, 29–41.

Chase, L. J., and Tucker, R. K. (1976). Statistical power: Derivation, development, and data-analytic implications. *Psychological Record, 26*, 473–486.

Chen, H. T., & Rossi, P. H. (1981). The multi-goal, theory-driven approach to evaluation: A model linking basic and applied social science. In H. E. Freeman & M. A. Soloman (Eds.), *Evaluation studies review annual* (Vol. 6, pp. 38–54). Beverly Hills, CA: Sage.

Clark, R. (1974). *A study of the power of research as reported in the Journal for Research in Mathematics Education.* Unpublished doctoral dissertation, University of Tennessee, Memphis.

Cleary, T. A., & Linn, R. L. (1969). Error of measurement and the power of a statistical test. *The British Journal of Mathematical and Statistical Psychology, 22,* 49–55.

Cleary, T. A., Linn, R. L., & Walster, G. W. (1970). Effect of reliability and validity on power of statistical tests. In E. F. Borgatta & G. W. Bohrnstedt (Eds.), *Sociological methodology* (pp. 130–138). San Francisco: Jossey-Bass.

Cohen, J. (1962). The statistical power of abnormal-social psychological research: A review. *Journal of Abnormal and Social Psychology, 65,* 145–153.

Cohen, J. (1970). Approximate power and sample size determination for common one-sample and two-sample hypothesis tests. *Educational and Psychological Measurement, 30,* 811–831.

Cohen, J. (1977). *Statistical power analysis for the behavioral sciences* (rev. ed.). New York: Academic Press.

Cohen, J. (1983). The cost of dichotomization. *Applied Psychological Measurement, 7,* 249–253.

Cohen, J. (1988). *Statistical power analysis for the behavioral sciences* (2nd ed.). Hillsdale, NJ: Lawrence Erlbaum.

Cohen, J., & Cohen, P. (1975). *Applied multiple regression/correlation analysis for the behavioral sciences.* Hillsdale, NJ: Lawrence Erlbaum.

Cohen, P. (1982). To be or not to be: Control and balancing of Type I and Type II errors. *Evaluation and Program Planning, 5,* 247–253.

Coleman, J. S., Campbell, E. Q., Hobson, C. J., McPartland, J., Mood, A. M., Weinfeld, F. D., & York, R. L. (1966). *Equality of educational opportunity* (No. FS5.238:38001). Washington, DC: U.S. Government Printing Office.

Cook, T. D., & Campbell, D. T. (1979). *Quasi-experimentation: Design and analysis issues for field settings.* Chicago: Rand McNally.

Cook, T. J., & Poole, W. K. (1982). Treatment implementation and statistical power. *Evaluation Review, 6,* 425–430.

Cordray, D. S., & Orwin, R. G. (1983). Improving the quality of evidence: Interconnections among primary evaluation, secondary analysis, and quantitative synthesis. In R. J. Light (Ed.), *Evaluation studies review annual* (Vol. 8, pp. 91–119). Beverly Hills, CA: Sage.

Cordray, D. S., & Sonnefeld, L. J. (1985). Quantitative synthesis: An actuarial base for planning impact evaluations. *New Directions for Program Evaluation, 27,* 29–48.

Cronbach, L. J., Gleser, G. C., Nanda, H., & Rajaratnam, N. (1972). *The dependability of behavioral measurements: Theory of generalizability for scores and profiles.* New York: John Wiley.

Dixon, W. F., & Massey, F. J. (1957). *Introduction to statistical analysis* (2nd ed.). New York: McGraw-Hill.

Epstein, S. (1980). The stability of behavior II. Implications for psychological research. *American Psychologist, 35,* 790–806.

Fischer, J. (1978). Does anything work? *Journal of Social Service Research, 1,* 215–243.

Glass, G. V., McGaw, B., & Smith, M. L. (1981). *Meta-analysis in social research.* Beverly Hills, CA: Sage.

Green, R. S., Nguyen, T. D., & Attkisson, C. C. (1979). Harnessing the reliability of outcome measures. *Evaluation and Program Planning, 2,* 137–142.

Guilford, J. P. (1954). Theory of psychological tests. In *Psychometric methods* (pp. 341–372). New York: McGraw-Hill.

Gulliksen, H. (1950). *Theory of mental tests.* New York: John Wiley.

Haladyna, T., & Roid, G. (1981). The role of instructional sensitivity in the empirical review of criterion-referenced test items. *Journal of Educational Measurement, 18,* 39–53.

Hanna, G. S., & Bennett, J. A. (1984). Instructional sensitivity expanded. *Educational and Psychological Measurement, 44,* 583–596.

Hays, W. L. (1973). *Statistics for the social sciences* (2nd ed.). New York: Holt, Rinehart, & Winston.

Hedges, L. V., & Olkin, I. (1985). *Statistical methods for meta-analysis.* New York: Academic Press.

Holmes, C. T. (1984). Effect size estimation in meta-analysis. *The Journal of Experimental Education, 52,* 106–109.

Howard, K. I., Kopta, S. M., Krause, M. S., & Orlinsky, D. E. (1986). The dose-effect relationship in psychotherapy. *American Psychologist, 41,* 159–164.

Hunter, J. E. (1987). Multiple dependent variables in program evaluation. *New Directions for Program Evaluation, 35,* 43–56.

Hunter, J. E., Schmidt, F. C., & Jackson, G. B. (1982). *Meta-analysis: Cumulating research findings across studies.* Beverly Hills, CA: Sage.

Judd, C. M., & Kenny, D. A. (1981). Process analysis: Estimating mediation in treatment evaluations. *Evaluation Review, 5,* 602–619.

Kelly, J. R., & McGrath, J. E. (1988). *On time and method.* Newbury Park, CA: Sage.

Kirk, R. W. (1982). *Experimental design: Procedures for the behavioral sciences* (2nd ed.). Monterey, CA: Brooks/Cole.

Kraemer, H. C., & Thiemann, S. (1987). *How many subjects? Statistical power analysis in research.* Newbury Park, CA: Sage.

Kroll, R. M., & Chase, L. J. (1975). Communication disorders: A power analytic assessment of recent research. *Journal of Communication Disorders, 8,* 237–247.

Levenson, R. I. (1980). Statistical power analysis: Implications for researchers, planners, and practitioners in gerontology. *The Gerontologist, 20,* 494–498.

Levin, J. R., & Subkoviak, M. J. (1977). Planning an experiment in the company of measurement error. *Applied Psychological Measurement, 1,* 331–338.

Levin, J. R., & Subkoviak, M. J. (1978). Correcting "Planning an experiment in the company of measurement error." *Applied Psychological Measurement, 2,* 382–385.

Lipsey, M. W. (1982). *Measurement issues in the evaluation of the effects of juvenile delinquency programs* (Project 80-IJ-CX-0036). Washington, DC: National Institute of Justice, Office of Research and Evaluation Methods, National Criminal Justice Reference Service Document No. NCJ-84968.

Lipsey, M. W. (1983). A scheme for assessing measurement sensitivity in program evaluation and other applied research. *Psychological Bulletin, 94,* 152–165.

Lipsey, M. W. (1990). Theory as method: Small theories of treatments. In L. Sechrest, J. Bunker, & E. Perrin (Eds.), *Health services research methodology: Strengthening causal inference from nonexperimental research.* Washington, DC: U. S. Public Health Service, National Center for Health Services Research and Health Care Technology Research.

Lipsey, M. W., Cordray, D. S., & Berger, D. E. (1981). Evaluation of a juvenile diversion program: Using multiple lines of evidence. *Evaluation Review, 5,* 283–306.

Lipsey, M. W., Crosse, S., Dunkle, J., Pollard, J., & Stobart, G. (1985). Evaluation: The state of the art and the sorry state of the science. *New Directions for Program Evaluation*, *27*, 7–28.

Mark, M. M. (1983). Treatment implementation, statistical power, and internal validity. *Evaluation Review*, *4*, 543–549.

Maxwell, S. E., Delaney, H. D., & Dill, C. A. (1984). Another look at ANCOVA versus blocking. *Psychological Bulletin*, *95*, 136–147.

Mazen, A. M., Graf, L. A., Kellogg, C. E., & Hemmasi, M. (1987). Statistical power in contemporary management research. *Academy of Management Journal*, *30*, 369–380.

Mazzeo, J., & Seeley, G. W. (1984). A general framework for evaluating the reliability of medical measurement systems. *Evaluation and the Health Professions*, *7*, 379–411.

Mosteller, F., Gilbert, J. P., & McPeek, B. (1980). Reporting standards and research strategies for controlled trials: Agenda for the editor. *Controlled Clinical Trials*, *1*, 37–58.

Myers, J. L. (1979). *Fundamentals of experimental design*. Boston: Allyn & Bacon.

Nagel, S. S., & Neef, M. (1977). Determining an optimum level of statistical significance. In M. Guttentag & S. Saar (Eds.), *Evaluation studies review annual* (Vol. 2, pp. 146–158). Beverly Hills, CA: Sage.

Nitko, A. J. (1980). Distinguishing the many varieties of criterion-referenced tests. *Review of Educational Research*, *50*, 461–485.

Ottenbacher, K. (1982). Statistical power and research in occupational therapy. *Occupational Therapy Journal of Research*, *2*, 13–25.

Owen, D. B. (1962). *Handbook of statistical tables*. Reading, MA: Addison-Wesley.

Owen, D. B. (1965). The power of student's t-test. *Journal of the American Statistical Association*, *60*, 320–333.

Ozer, D. J. (1985). Correlation and the coefficient of determination. *Psychological Bulletin*, *97*, 307–315.

Popham, W. J. (1978). *Criterion-referenced measurement*. Englewood Cliffs, NJ: Prentice-Hall.

Prather, J. E., & Gibson, F. K. (1977). The failure of social programs. *Public Administration Review*, *37*, 556–564.

Reed, J. F., & Slaichert, W. (1981). Statistical proof in inconclusive 'negative' trials. *Archives of Internal Medicine*, *141*, 1307–1310.

Reichardt, C. S., & Gollob, H. F. (1987). Taking uncertainty into account when estimating effects. *New Directions for Program Evaluation*, *35*, 7–22.

Rezmovic, E. L., Cook, T. J., & Dobson, L. D. (1981). Beyond random assignment: Factors affecting evaluation integrity. *Evaluation Review*, *5*, 51–67.

Rosenthal, R. (1984). *Meta-analytic procedures for social research*. Beverly Hills, CA: Sage.

Rosenthal, R., & Rubin, D. B. (1982). A simple, general purpose display of magnitude of experimental effect. *Journal of Educational Psychology*, *74*, 166–169.

Rossi, P. H., & Wright, J. D. (1984). Evaluation research: An assessment. *Annual Review of Sociology*, *10*, 331–352.

Sawyer, A., & Ball, A. (1981). Statistical power and effect size in marketing research. *Journal of Marketing Research*, *18*, 275–290.

Schery, T. K. (1981). Selecting assessment strategies for language disordered children. *Topics in Language Disorders*, *1*, 59–73.

Schneider, A. L., & Darcy, R. E. (1984). Policy implications of using significance tests in evaluation research. *Evaluation Review*, *8*, 573–582.

Schwartz, J. E. (1985). The neglected problem of measurement error in categorical data. *Sociological Methods and Research, 13,* 435–466.

Sechrest, L., & Yeaton, W. H. (1981). Empirical bases for estimating effect size. In R. F. Boruch, P. M. Wortman, D. S. Cordray, & Associates (Eds.), *Reanalyzing program evaluations: Policies and practices for secondary analysis of social and educational programs* (pp. 212–224). San Francisco: Jossey-Bass.

Sechrest, L., & Yeaton, W. H. (1982). Magnitudes of experimental effects in social science research. *Evaluation Review, 6,* 579–600.

Siegel, S. (1956). *Nonparametric statistics.* New York: McGraw-Hill.

Smith, M. L., & Glass, G. V. (1977). Meta-analysis of psychotherapy outcome studies. *American Psychologist, 32,* 752–760.

Smith, M. L., Glass, G. V., & Miller, T. I. (1980). *The benefits of psychotherapy.* Baltimore: Johns Hopkins University Press.

Spreitzer, E. (1974). *Statistical power in sociological research: An examination of data-analytic strategies.* Unpublished manuscript, Department of Sociology, Bowling Green State University.

Stanley, J. C. (1971). Reliability. In R. L. Thorndike (Ed.), *Educational measurement* (2nd ed., pp. 356–442). Washington, DC: American Council on Education.

Subkoviak, M. J., & Levin, J. R. (1977). Fallibility of measurement and the power of a statistical test. *Journal of Educational Measurement, 14,* 47–52.

Wang, M. C., & Walberg, H. J. (1983). Evaluating educational programs: An integrative, casual-modeling approach. *Educational Evaluation and Policy Analysis, 5,* 347–366.

Wilkins, W. (1986). Placebo problems in psychotherapy research: Social-psychological alternatives to chemotherapy concepts. *American Psychologist, 41,* 551–556.

Winer, B. J. (1971). *Statistical principles in experimental design.* New York: McGraw-Hill.

Yeaton, W. H., & Sechrest, L. (1981). Critical dimensions in the choice and maintenance of successful treatments: Strength, integrity, and effectiveness. *Journal of Consulting and Clinical Psychology, 49,* 156–167.

Author Index

Subject Index

Printed in the United States
42778LVS00002B/163-180

9 780803 930636

About the Author

Mark W. Lipsey is a Professor of Psychology at The Claremont Graduate School, one of the six affiliated institutions of the Claremont Colleges and University Center at Claremont, California. He received a B.S. in applied psychology from the Georgia Institute of Technology in 1968 and a Ph.D. in (social) psychology from The Johns Hopkins University in 1972.

Professor Lipsey's academic career has been devoted to expanding the role of psychologists in research on important social issues and organizations. He is one of the architects of the innovative graduate program in applied and public affairs psychology at Claremont Graduate School and has served as its chairman for the last five years. His own research has focused on planned intervention and methods for assessing its effects in such areas as juvenile delinquency, social services, and environment. His current interests include meta-analysis of delinquency treatment research, investigation of what meta-analysis reveals generally about treatment effectiveness research in the behavioral sciences, and methodological innovations in field experimentation.

Professor Lipsey has served as Editor-in-Chief of *New Directions for Program Evaluation* (a journal of the American Evaluation Association) and edited (with David Cordray) the 1986 volume of *Evaluation Studies Review Annual*. He was a Fulbright Lecturer to the University of Delhi in 1985–86 and has been a consultant for a variety of projects in juvenile justice, mental health, social services, healthcare, environment, and education.